"This book is the ultimate guide to hospitali_____
way I approach hosting and hang-ups I've ha__ ___ ___ to work through them to become better at it. Morgan explains everything in a relatable way while giving actionable steps that work best for my personality."

Mique Provost, owner, Thirty Handmade Days

"Morgan does such a beautiful job helping us discover that we are all wired for hospitality and that there is no one way to be hospitable. Her book felt like the enneagram meets the host. I loved discovering more about what type of hospitality personality I have, and Morgan made me feel understood and confident with her practical suggestions to show up, host, and make others feel seen."

Sarah Bragg, host of *Surviving Sarah* and *Raising Boys & Girls* podcasts

"Knowing we should be hospitable and actually being hospitable are two different things. This book shows us that no matter our hospitality personality, people tolerance, or giftedness, we all can open up our lives and homes to others in a way that complements our everyday lives. This is perhaps what I love the most about Morgan's writing. She is able to take a big idea, like hospitality, and apply it to real-life examples, modern schedules, and doable actions. Loaded with practical ideas, this book will inspire you to open the door and open your heart!"

Krista Gilbert, author of *Reclaiming Home*, speaker, and cohost of *The Open Door Sisterhood* podcast and Home Coach

"Hospitality is near and dear to my heart. Yet I know that I'm wired differently than others in how I approach opening my home. Extending hospitality doesn't have to fit a particular mold, and Morgan helps us all to understand and embrace our natural differences. We can relax and enjoy opening our homes and do it in a way that fits with our natural strengths. *Your Hospitality Personality* is filled with practical advice and how-tos for hosting that will make any reader feel more confident in practicing hospitality."

Kristi Clover, author of *M.O.M.=Master Organizer of Mayhem* and host of the *Simply Joyful* podcast

"I am always fascinated by looking at different topics through the lens of personality types, and hospitality is no exception! Morgan does a great job of making hospitality feel accessible to everyone, no matter where their individual strengths lie. So often we feel as if hospitality has to look one certain way, but Morgan proves that hospitality can have many faces and that nearly everyone can find a way to incorporate it into their lives!"

Abby Lawson, author and creator at *Just a Girl and Her Blog* and Abby Organizes

"As someone who claims a multi–hospitality personality, I was motivated to fully embrace who I am in terms of hospitality by Morgan Tyree's gentle enlightenment, encouragement, and practical tips. No longer do I get overwhelmed by trying and doing and being all things; instead, I'm a more relaxed and enjoyable host because of this book. I recommend *Your Hospitality Personality* for the person who wants to open up their life, just as it is, and connect more deeply with others."

Kristin Funston, speaker and author of *More for Mom: Living Your Whole and Holy Life*

"This book is an open-door invitation on how to naturally connect with others. Morgan reminds us that hospitality isn't reserved for dinner parties. It can look like meeting friends for coffee or bringing someone a meal. I love how Morgan identifies four unique hospitality styles and offers suggestions and examples throughout the book of how to use our unique gifts to serve others. It was such an easy read that I felt as though I was having a conversation with a girlfriend!"

Laurie Palau, founder of Simply B Organized, host of the weekly podcast *This ORGANIZED Life*, and author of *Hot Mess: A Practical Guide to Getting Organized*

"In a world where taking the time to show hospitality seems like a lost art, Morgan reminds us what is truly important—connection with other people. This book hits right at the heart and teaches you to host without fear and with confidence, no matter what the occasion!"

Brandie Larsen and Ryan Eiesland, founders of Home Sort and the How To Summit

your hospitality personality

your hospitality personality

How to Confidently
Create Connection and Community

MORGAN TYREE

Revell

a division of Baker Publishing Group
Grand Rapids, Michigan

© 2020 by Morganize with Me, LLC

Published by Revell
a division of Baker Publishing Group
PO Box 6287, Grand Rapids, MI 49516-6287
www.revellbooks.com

Printed in the United States of America

Library of Congress Cataloging-in-Publication Data
Names: Tyree, Morgan, author.
Title: Your hospitality personality : how to confidently create connection and community / Morgan Tyree.
Description: Grand Rapids, Michigan : Revell, a division of Baker Publishing Group, 2020. | Includes bibliographical references.
Identifiers: LCCN 2019039576 | ISBN 9780800736927 (paperback)
Subjects: LCSH: Hospitality—Religious aspects—Christianity. | Personality—Religious aspects—Christianity.
Classification: LCC BV4647.H67 T97 2020 | DDC 241/.671—dc23
LC record available at https://lccn.loc.gov/2019039576

The author is represented by the literary agency of The Blythe Daniel Agency, Inc.

20 21 22 23 24 25 26   7 6 5 4 3 2 1

To Julie Davis—
When I think of hospitality,
I think of you.

contents

Acknowledgments   13

Part 1 Your Hospitality Heartbeat

1. Welcome!   17
2. The Four Hospitality Personalities   22

Part 2 Your Hospitality Habits

3. Setting: Open Home or Closed Home   43
4. Scheduling: Planning or Spontaneity   51
5. Serving: Foodie or Non-Foodie   58
6. Socializing: Extrovert, Introvert, or Ambivert   66
7. Sharing: Giving or Receiving   73

Part 3 Your Hospitality Hurdles

8. Who: Circles   83
9. What: Experience   94
10. Where: Venue   101
11. When: Time   109
12. Why: Love   115

Part 4 Your Hospitality Hang-Ups

13. Connection: Fellowship and Fumbles   123

14. Collaboration: Food and Finances   135

15. Coziness: Fanciness and Function   143

Part 5 Your Hospitality Help

16. Hosting Tips: How-To   155

17. Hosting Themes: DIY   171

Conclusion: Open Your Heart   193

Notes   195

Be a pineapple:
Stand tall,
wear a crown,
and be sweet on the inside.

Katherine Gaskin

acknowledgments

A creative project like this one takes a team, and I want to offer my heartfelt appreciation to the following:

My husband—David, for reading every word, challenging me, and listening well. Having you as my sounding board and my hosting partner is an absolute gift.

My children—Ainsley, Connor, and Berkley, you three light up my life. Thank you for your ongoing encouragement and support. Your cheers for me mean the most!

My parents—Steve and Janet, for your outstanding examples of hospitality. Thank you for loving others well and inspiring me to do the same.

My sisters—Haley, for your ability to make things cozy and your constant support; and Harmony, for introducing me to charcuterie boards and always having fresh flowers when I visit.

My friends—Marta, Ashley, Jamie, Julie D., Tami, Bonnie, Christy, Nick, and Kristen, for allowing me to include your wonderful stories of hospitality. I am deeply grateful for our friendship and connection.

My hosting team—Bri, Janet, Inger, Haley, Jill, Julie P., Tammy, Kimbra, Julie C., Julie D., Krista, Kate, April, Abby, and Jennie, for sharing your fabulous tips, themes, recipes, and more! This last section was the sweet ending to this wonderful project.

My editors—Andrea Doering, for trusting me to shape and share this beautiful message; and Gisèle Mix, for helping to proof and perfect my words so graciously.

My publishing team—for your tremendous help and support. I'd be lost without you!

My agent—Blythe Daniel, for always being my advocate and believing in me.

My community—readers, listeners, and clients, for joining with me, encouraging me, and desiring to live intentionally and purposefully.

PART 1

your
hospitality
heartbeat

True hospitality consists of
giving the best of yourself
to your guests.

Eleanor Roosevelt

CHAPTER ONE

welcome!

Welcome! I'm so glad you are here. Please come in and make yourself at home. My hope is that you will feel comfortable and cozy as we chat about hospitality. You are welcome to grab a blanket, put your feet up, and settle into my worn leather couch. What can I get you to drink? Would you like coffee, tea, water? I want you to feel relaxed and at home during our time together.

Extending hospitality can mean different things to different people. It might look like a new neighbor dropping off a "welcome" basket filled with goodies on your move-in day. Someone may offer to help do dishes after sharing a meal together. You could hold the door open for the person behind you. A friend may extend an invitation to gather together for a celebration on a special occasion. Sometimes it's as simple as offering a warm smile to your cashier or to a stranger you pass on the street.

Hospitality is a gift that is both given and received. For some it comes naturally, and for others it may be a gift reserved for special occasions. Some may feel they aren't able to offer hospitality, perhaps because of lack of practice, time, or resources. However, I believe every person can learn how to extend hospitality.

We are created and designed to be in community. "Connection is why we're here. We are hardwired to connect with others, it's what gives purpose and meaning to our lives, and without it there is suffering."[1] From storytelling around a fire to sharing on social media, our desire to be known and in meaningful relationships is a universal heartfelt need. Nonetheless, that yearning to do life with others can be hindered by our fears and insecurities. These reservations usually manifest in our personalities, which can limit our attempts to share who we are.

While I enjoy many parts of hospitality, I also have plenty of struggles when it comes to hosting. I'm no Giada De Laurentiis, Julia Child, Martha Stewart, or whoever you may look to as someone who resembles a "hostess with the mostest" persona. I love the planning and preparing, the details and decisions, and even the anticipation. However, I don't like the pressure of cleaning, shopping, and coordinating the timing and execution of everything. Can you relate? Are there parts of hosting you like and parts you would rather avoid altogether? Are there areas that feel natural to you and others that feel completely foreign? Do you vacillate between feeling eager and hesitant to host?

On the hosting continuum, we all land somewhere between reluctant and ready. Reluctant hosting means you tend to feel hesitant when extending an invite or hosting a gathering. Ready hosting means you tend to feel energized and motivated when planning to host or coordinate social activities. Wherever you fall on the hosting continuum, you have a hospitality personality, and it impacts how you approach hosting.

> You have a hospitality personality, and it impacts how you approach hosting.

Your hospitality personality describes the heart behind how you respond internally and externally to your opportunities to connect with others. It is the style in which you prefer to host and points to the ways of hosting that feel the most comfortable and natural to you. Your hospitality personality is part of your hardwiring and is what makes you, you. It has been molded, developed, and influenced by a variety of factors: your family of origin, your circles of influence, and the different cultures and experiences you've been exposed to. As we explore your hospitality personality, you will learn your natural personality type—and how to develop new tools and techniques to encourage and equip you as a host.

Whether organizing, decorating, cooking, baking, cleaning, serving, creating, or socializing, hospitality can feel exhausting and overwhelming. Hosting can be hard work and can rob you of the enjoyment of the event regardless of whether you feel like a reluctant or a ready host, but it doesn't have to. The beauty in knowing, understanding, and embracing your hospitality personality is that you can become an even better and more relaxed host. Discerning the reasons behind why and how you host will help you to better understand and address your hospitality habits, hurdles, and hang-ups.

As you journey through this book, you will recognize your natural hosting habits and how to train up your strengths and work through your weaknesses. With hosting, like playing music at a party, it's all about knowing your audience and finding the right volume. You, as the host, set the tone. You can establish your own healthy habits and emphasize a tone of authenticity. Whether hosting a dinner for eight, a book club gathering, a child's birthday party, a graduation celebration, or a girls' night out, hospitality requires vulnerability—and vulnerability takes courage! Inviting people into your home, coordinating a gathering, or reaching out to someone opens you up to receiving feedback, solicited or otherwise, and it's not always positive. However, I believe that when you create a safe space for everyone to be vulnerable, you can focus on building connection rather than entertaining unwelcome feelings of comparison or competition. You can create a cozy space where your guests feel comfortable and cared for just as they are.

Once you've identified your habits, you'll consider your hospitality hurdles. In other words, what obstacles keep you from wanting to host? What parts of hosting feel more like hindrances to you? There are so many questions to address: *Who do I invite? What do we do? Where do we do it? When do we do it? Why are we doing it?* You'll ask yourself where you tend to get stuck and which of these interferences may seem like too much trouble. Hospitality hurdles can stop you from being inclined to host, but they don't have to! They can instead motivate you and help you to grow as a host.

After clearing your hospitality hurdles, you'll discover how to maneuver through the inevitable hospitality hang-ups—those things that keep you from enjoying your time when hosting, such as menu planning, hosting on a budget, making your home or space function well, or meeting other people's obligations while also being true to yourself. Exploring how to minimize your personal hesitations will enable you to more confidently bring people together and enjoy your time with others to the fullest.

Through this quest, you'll be inspired to keep on mission with your hopes for hosting. There will be more blessing and less stressing as you learn how to observe modern-day manners and handle common hospitality difficulties. Also included in the book are down-to-earth, real-life party ideas. I asked some amazing hostesses from all hospitality personalities to share their hosting secrets with you. The guesswork is gone; you can turn to their tried-and-true hosting tips and themes and have all of the prep work done for you! You're welcome.

God calls us to be hospitable. Hospitality is an act of love, and most of all, an opportunity to build connection. It tells others you care, you want to build community, and you desire friendship. I pray you will welcome your unique and God-given hospitality personality and host in the ways that best complement your style.

That you will have a fresh perspective of what hospitality can and should look like—for you. Ultimately, that you will be able to more fully live your mission, love your people, and create the space and time for true connection.

Your hospitality personality is a gift—the present of being present. Make sure to give it away!

CHAPTER TWO

the four hospitality personalities

As a hostess, I lean toward making things easy for myself. I'm a *less is more* kind of person. I've also learned that when I have too many time-intensive tasks on my hosting to-do list, I become burdened by my list and tend toward feeling anxious or even resentful. Therefore, I work to balance my list with a reasonable number of tasks and streamline things whenever and wherever I can. When we have people over to share a meal, I'll opt to serve ice cream for dessert, select a premade dinner salad, ask our guests to bring an appetizer, and almost always rely on one of my tried-and-true (super simple) main dish recipes. I rarely look at the opportunity to host as a time to be adventurous or to try new things. Instead, I create a plan that is comfortable for me and one that will make my guests feel comfortable too. My hosting style centers on simplicity.

When we lived overseas, our pastor's wife asked me to bring an appetizer to her husband's birthday party. She specifically requested I bring a vegetable platter with a "ranch" dip. This was music to my ears—easy, easy, easy! I quickly responded with a "Yes!" Ranch dip, to me, is the store-bought, premade Hidden

Valley Ranch powder mix combined with sour cream. I prepared a simple veggie tray with the desired ranch dip and brought it to the party on a pretty serving platter. Now for context, this was an international birthday party with mostly Portuguese guests, and my veggie tray attracted some major attention. Which was a surprise to me. Who would have thought that some carrots and celery could draw a crowd?

I was bombarded with questions: "What is this sauce?" "How did you make this?" And my favorite of all—"Which spices did you use in this dip?" I found myself trying to list some of the possible spices that might be in the premade mix. I responded with, "I think there is some parsley, salt, maybe a little garlic . . ." I was searching for answers to a roomful of inquisitive Portuguese people. I had never been pressed for a recipe like this before! Especially a recipe that included ingredients listed in great length on the side of a *cardboard box*. I did my best to explain that the dip was made from a store-bought premade mix and I had just combined it with a container of sour cream. This didn't help much because I had purchased the mix and sour cream from our American commissary, which was not a shopping option accessible to the investigating partygoers.

It was amusing to me that my understated and unimpressive veggie tray was a huge hit. There was even a chef in attendance who loved it and wanted to re-create it. So yes, I inspired a chef! There's a first time for everything, I guess! Which just goes to show that even the smallest attempt at hospitality can be a huge success. My emphasis on simplicity didn't set me back at all.

Here's the beauty of hosting, regardless of its simplicity or complexity: every single person has the ability to learn the art of hospitality. Whether you are serving as a host or socializing as a guest, you have a special and unique hospitality personality. You are designed in such a beautiful way, and it's important to remember this truth. You were created with a heart that desires to connect with others and to be in community. As human beings, we need to *be* with others. By joining with others, we feel less isolated and alone. We feel known and loved.

The dictionary defines *hospitality* as "the friendly reception and treatment of guests or strangers, the quality or disposition of receiving and treating guests and strangers in a warm, friendly, generous way."[1] *Personality* is defined as "the visible aspects of one's character as it impresses others: a person as an embodiment of a collection of qualities."[2]

Hospitality is what you do, and personality is how you do it.

Your hospitality personality is the style in which you prefer to socialize and the ways of hosting that feel the most comfortable and natural to you. It's the heartbeat behind how and why you host. Knowing, understanding—and maybe most importantly embracing—your hospitality personality is the key to fully experiencing the joys of hosting and socializing too! So let's dive into your hospitality personality.

Please select only **one** *answer per question—the one that sounds like you most of the time.*

1. **What do you tend to do at parties?**
   a. look for ways to help facilitate and lead things
   b. find myself telling stories and meeting lots of new people
   c. notice the decor, appreciate the menu, and savor the experience
   d. see all of the details that went into the party and try to help where I can

2. **When hosting a gathering, what do you like to do?**
   a. start new traditions and bring people together
   b. have fun and relax
   c. create a beautiful atmosphere
   d. take care of as much as I can beforehand

24

3. **What size group do you prefer at get-togethers?**
    a. whatever size required
    b. the more the merrier
    (c.) one that connects naturally and feels comfortable together
    d. smaller and more intimate

4. **How often do you like to gather with friends and family?**
    (a.) as often as my schedule allows
    b. daily—if possible
    c. regularly—at least weekly if not more
    d. as much as we can plan and get it scheduled

5. **How does hosting make you feel?**
    a. charged
    (b.) energized
    c. connected
    d. organized

6. **Which words best describe you?**
    a. leader and delegator
    b. socializer and entertainer
    c. relator and creator
    (d.) planner and refiner

7. **When you go for a walk, what do you like to do?**
    a. walk at a fast pace on the treadmill and listen to a podcast
    (b.) walk in my neighborhood and talk on the phone
    c. walk to my local coffee shop and meet a good friend for coffee
    d. walk to the library and look for a new book to read

8. *How would you describe your personal fashion style?*
   a. mix of colors, neutrals, and great accessories
   b. lots of options with plenty of colors and prints
   c. casual, stylish, and on trend
   d. mostly basics and classics

9. *What motivates you?*
   a. success
   b. competition
   c. relationships
   d. goals

10. *Of the following activities, what would you choose?*
    a. exploring a new place
    b. adventuring outdoors
    c. spending time with family and/or friends
    d. reading a book or watching a movie

11. *If you were to throw a theme party, which theme would you choose?*
    a. ugly sweater and charity giveaway
    b. totally awesome '80s party
    c. something I found on Pinterest
    d. game or movie night

12. *When you have a free day, how do you like to spend it?*
    a. doing a hobby—gardening, decorating, exercising, cooking, and so on
    b. doing something fun
    c. visiting or shopping with a friend
    d. reorganizing my closet or working on my to-do list

13. *How do you respond to stress?*

a. It makes me take more risks.

b. It motivates me.

c. It overwhelms me.

d. It focuses me.

14. *How would you define your home's style?*

a. stylish and traditional

b. casual and relaxed

c. cozy and warm

d. streamlined and minimal

15. *At a dinner table, where do you prefer to sit?*

a. at the head

b. anywhere

c. middle

d. corner

16. *Do you procrastinate?*

a. not really

b. always

c. sometimes

d. never

17. *If your weekend plans fall through, what are you most likely to do?*

a. make new plans immediately

b. see what happens

c. call a friend

d. feel relieved that I now have more free time

18. **When you go to a social gathering, what do you do?**

    a. dive into conversation

    b. jump right into telling stories

    c. look for someone to connect with

    d. see if there is something I can do to help

19. **What do you prefer when it comes to cooking, menu planning, and food prep?**

    a. I rely more on takeout and outsourcing than on doing it myself.

    b. I love to come up with my own inspired dishes, on the fly.

    c. I enjoy cooking and love preparing new menus.

    d. I can cook, but I don't consider it a hobby.

Tally up the number of times you answered each letter, fill in the numbers below, and then circle the one with the highest number (primary) and the second-highest number (secondary).

A: _____   C: _____

B: _____   D: _____

What is your hospitality personality?

If you answered mostly As, then you have the hospitality personality of a Leader.

If you answered mostly Bs, then you have the hospitality personality of an Entertainer.

If you answered mostly Cs, then you have the hospitality personality of an Includer.

If you answered mostly Ds, then you have the hospitality personality of an Organizer.

Your primary hospitality personality is: _____

Your secondary hospitality personality is: _____

Please note the quiz is arranged to help you identify where you tend to be *most of the time* and where you are most likely to *hang out* when serving in the role as either host or guest. At times, you will move between types and you may find that in different groups and/ or settings you switch to different styles of engagement. However, your primary and secondary hospitality personalities are where you feel the most authentically yourself when socializing or hosting.

The goal is to embrace your hospitality personality and realize how you respond in a default sort of way. Hospitality ultimately encompasses all of the personality styles, and all four aspects are important to hosting: leading, entertaining, including, and organizing. However, by acknowledging your hospitality personality, you can learn how to host in the ways that best align with who you are naturally.

There is no reason to try to be someone you are not, especially when hosting. When that happens, you as a host are not who you really are to your guest(s). When you are secure in who you are, you host best. Insecurities reveal tensions and can often limit intimacy rather than foster it. The more secure and confident you are, the deeper you'll be able to connect with others. Your authenticity and vulnerability will, in turn, invite others to be authentic and vulnerable too.

Leader: "The Director"

If you ask a Leader to host, they will promptly start delegating and doing!

You are a born leader. You like to be in charge, and you feel confident with calling the shots—not in a bossy sort of way but in a *"let's get things done"* sort of way. People regularly look to you to grab the reins and get things started. You enjoy hosting and are extremely good at delegating and leading the charge. You may have a few go-to recipes, opt for premade or catered options, or gravitate toward creating an elaborate menu and using your gourmet cooking skills. You are a natural when it comes to seeing the big picture of an event and knowing what it will take to pull it off. You lead gatherings well and hospitality is something you do almost seamlessly.

As a Leader, some of your strengths might look like this:

- *You're decisive and confident.* You don't tend to vacillate and you know what you want.
- *You're focused, strong-willed, and assertive.* In the best possible way! As a natural leader, you get things done—yesterday!
- *You're logical, practical, and disciplined.* You are highly motivated and know how to prioritize and delegate well, and that's why you are the one usually in charge.

You may exhibit some of these weaknesses:

- *You're impatient.* Because you're highly motivated it can sometimes be hard for you to remain patient within the process.
- *You're competitive and focused.* You have a high level of performance standards for yourself and others.
- *You're opinionated and driven.* Your way is sometimes the only way.

Entertainer: "The Socializer"

If you ask an Entertainer to host, they will be thrilled, tell everyone about the event, and then wait to prepare everything at the last minute. (And yes, still manage to pull it off!)

You are the life of the party. You love spending time socializing with others. You are not hyperfocused about the details but you are definitely the one people count on for the laughter and jokes. You love telling stories and talking to new people. Social settings are typically very energizing for you. You are happy to whip up a meal and don't take yourself too seriously about any of the specifics of hosting. You are always up for all things social, and if someone hands you a mic or asks you to join them on the dance floor, you usually don't hesitate. You are naturally laid-back— less concerned about the details and more concerned about the dynamics. People want you at their parties because you bring the fun!

As an Entertainer, some of your strengths might look like this:

- *You're optimistic and spontaneous.* Positivity and living in the moment describe you through and through.
- *You're inspirational and motivational.* Your energy and enthusiasm are very encouraging to others and pushes them to try to do new things.
- *You're expressive and passionate.* You feel things deeply and express them too! Your passion is contagious and often helps others to not take themselves so seriously.

You may exhibit some of these weaknesses:

- *You're impulsive and scattered.* Your planning skills are fairly relaxed and your routine is, well, not very routine.
- *You tend to not follow through.* You have lots of fabulous ideas but sometimes not a lot of follow-through with what you start.
- *You're disorganized.* Details are not your thing (generally) and you may tend to zigzag as you go about your to-do list (if you have one).

31

Includer: "The Supporter"

If you ask an Includer to host, they will quickly say yes, then might consider why they said yes, and then effortlessly rise to the occasion and pull off a fabulous event.

You naturally thrive in the arena of hosting. You appreciate all things centered on the table and find beauty in connection. You love creating a cozy atmosphere and making people feel loved and cared for. From pillows, to candles, to providing slippers for your guests, you love curating a warm and welcoming environment. You take pleasure in spending time cooking tasty dishes and then building memories around your table. You are determined to make people a priority and your loved ones know with certainty that they are a priority to you. You are all about bringing people together and nourishing their bodies and souls.

As an Includer, some of your strengths might look like this:

- *You're diplomatic and accepting.* You see things from both sides and are more about helping than hindering.
- *You're inclusive, welcoming, and nurturing.* Everyone feels embraced by you because you are warmhearted, encouraging, and loving. You also know how to read a room and are naturally sensitive to others.
- *You're devoted, concerned, and empathetic.* You have a big heart and it shows.

You may exhibit some of these weaknesses:

- *You're overwhelmed.* As more of a "yes" person, you may be prone to taking on more than you should or trying too hard to keep everyone happy.
- *You're sensitive and sentimental.* You are sometimes more focused on ideals than the "real," and this can lead to disappointment and/or hurt feelings.

- *You're complacent.* Sometimes your lack of preference or "go-along attitude" is one of your biggest challenges: you and your choices can tend to get forgotten or ignored.

Organizer: "The Planner"

If you ask an Organizer to host, they will check their schedule, graciously (or maybe a little reluctantly) agree, and then immediately get to work with the planning and coordinating.

You are a detailed host and planning *all the things* is your jam. You generally enjoy your hosting time more when you've done as much as you can beforehand. You automatically know what needs to be done and/or you make sure there is a structured plan in place. People look to you to take care of all the specifics. As a problem solver, you are always looking for ways to make sure that things run smoothly and efficiently. You often prefer smaller, more intimate settings and are not necessarily a fan of being put on the spot. Your guests appreciate your attention to detail and tend to feel more at ease because you've usually thought of just about everything!

As an Organizer, some of your strengths might look like this:

- *You're logical, practical, and detailed.* You see what needs to be done and you do it. You have a take-care-of-business mentality.
- *You're diligent, thorough, and consistent.* People know that you will handle things and follow through with what needs to be done (and on time).
- *You're responsible and quality focused.* You stay the course, stick to the plan, and have a knack for doing things 100 percent.

You may exhibit some of these weaknesses:

- *You tend to be a perfectionist.* Your high levels of discipline and focus may actually slow you down and/or keep you from enjoying your duties.
- *You can be critical or closed off.* With your soaring standards, you may be perceived as a threat to others because you can tend to appear that you have everything together.
- *You're indecisive.* You often mull things over, and this can make it hard for you to move forward decisively.

From the diagram, you can see that Leaders and Entertainers tend to lean toward extroversion, and Organizers and Includers tend to lean toward introversion. It doesn't matter whether you

HOSPITALITY PERSONALITIES

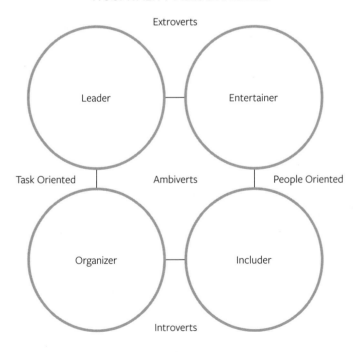

align more with being extroverted or introverted; both tendencies are gifts within how you share hospitality. Whichever way you tend to lean, or if you hover somewhere in the middle as more of an ambivert, lean into it. If you are more introverted, you are likely good at initiating one-on-one conversations. You probably have the keen ability to make someone feel accepted and welcomed by simply giving your attention and presence. If you are more extroverted, you might be a natural storyteller and are able to easily bring about laughter. In doing so, you help those around you to settle in and relax. Both are ways to help relieve tension and cultivate connection within social settings. Let it be a bridge to connect intentionally with others. Furthermore, Leaders and Organizers are more likely to be task oriented, and this is what makes them good at planning and executing! Entertainers and Includers are generally more people oriented. Their ability to make others feel welcomed and accepted is a notable strength. Recognizing what your natural tendencies are is helpful in knowing what strengths you bring to the table.

As you process the results of the quiz and the information about the four hospitality personalities, consider what your hospitality personality says about you as a host. Realize that each of these personalities has many strengths. That means YOU are equipped to be a great host! You just have your own style, which you should embrace. Isn't that refreshing? You have a heart of hospitality that is unique to you. You don't have to host like your mom, or your neighbor, or your best friend. You can simply host like YOU.

> Offer hospitality to one another without grumbling. Each of you should use whatever gift you have received to serve others, as faithful stewards of God's grace in its various forms. If anyone speaks, they should do so as one who speaks the very words of God. If anyone serves, they should do so with the strength God provides, so that in all things God may be praised through Jesus Christ. To him be the glory and the power for ever and ever. Amen. (1 Pet. 4:9–11)

Strengths and Weaknesses

I'm a primary Organizer and a secondary Includer. As an Organizer, I like to keep a tidy home and yes, my spices are organized alphabetically, but I've had to work to better develop some of my hospitality skills because I'm not necessarily shaped as a hostess with the mostest. I'm more introverted than extroverted, prefer calm to chaos, and don't necessarily like to spend a lot of time in my kitchen. Extending the invitation, welcoming people into my home, deciding what to do or what to serve—even reaching out to someone new—can all cause me more stress than bless. Thankfully, having a secondary side of being an Includer helps me to not take myself too seriously and to work to make people more of a priority than the details.

So maybe you've already guessed? Yes, I also tend to be more of a reluctant hostess than a ready one. However, despite feeling reluctant at times, I've decided what's most important is for me to work on being the most *relaxed* hostess I can be. To be a more relaxed host, I've learned to recognize my natural hosting strengths, such as being a good planner, organizer, and facilitator. I'm naturally detail-oriented and have a knack for thinking ahead and troubleshooting. I keep a color-coded calendar and am good with my time management. I don't mind stepping into a facilitating role and will take the lead if or when required. From hosting charity events, to work parties, to family holiday get-togethers, to kids' birthday parties, I've realized there are many parts of hosting that I do enjoy and that feel natural to me. As an Organizer, in the specific areas of planning, organizing, and facilitating I operate almost instinctively. Also, I'm really good at fluffing pillows, lighting candles, adding blankets, and stocking the pantry with plenty of treats—my Includer side helps here. (And these are all important things, if you ask me!)

The parts of hosting that are more challenging for me, or that can feel like weaknesses, are the aspects of entertaining, cooking, and creating. These parts of hosting are not as instinctive to me. I'm not usually the one to prepare a dinner playlist, be quick to tell a joke, or whip up a gourmet three-course meal. It's also easy for me to miss out on the fun of hosting because I can get overly focused on "doing" rather than "being." I can easily find myself feeling pressured to make sure that everyone is having a good time instead of me actively participating in the good time. I sometimes have to deliberately work to stay present rather than remaining productive. When I strike a healthy balance between my organizing side and my including side, I am usually able to better enjoy my time hosting and feel the most natural and relaxed.

To cater most effectively to your strengths and weaknesses, think in terms of flexibility. There are times to flex your strengths, and then there are moments when your weaknesses may allow others to flex their strengths. Self-awareness is the best way to maximize your strengths and minimize your weaknesses. By embracing my strengths *and* my weaknesses I've been able to welcome the vulnerability that comes with hosting and also more seamlessly steer through the inevitable challenges that accompany it. And trust me, there have been plenty of challenges!

> I sometimes have to deliberately work to stay present rather than remaining productive.

For example, there was that time I had a mini meltdown (in front of my guests) because my cheese queso didn't turn out for my daughter's Dora the Explorer–themed third birthday party. Apparently, you can *only* use the Velveeta brand of cheese when making this queso recipe. Well, I had been unable to find the "Velveeta cheese" because it wasn't where I thought it should be—*in the refrigerator section with the rest of the cheeses!* (This is coming from the girl who was raised on homemade yogurt and naturally ground peanut butter.) Did I mention this occurred in Albuquerque, New Mexico, the home of all things queso? Lesson learned. And despite the fact that we like to barbeque, we still don't own a set of steak knives. Which is why when recently serving steaks to our friends, I handed them a chef and a bread knife so that they could attempt to saw through their steaks! Then during a recent mini group "cooking lesson," I attempted to broil bread for an appetizer (for the first time, ever) and successfully burned the entire loaf. Is broiling really necessary? It seems overly complicated to me. The kitchen is not necessarily my wheelhouse. (Although I did just learn how to make coffee, so there's that.)

When problems arise—and they always seem to—I try to not take myself too seriously. I try to laugh at myself and stay relaxed (this is my Includer side talking). I believe that being relaxed as a host is key! Have you noticed that if you attend a get-together and the host is relaxed, then it's easier for you to also feel relaxed? *Relaxation is contagious!*

Regardless of your hospitality personality or whether you are a ready or reluctant host, you can maintain a sense of calm and create a relaxed gathering. Relaxed hosting looks like not being fearful of all the what-ifs, practicing being fully present, and not ignoring the desire you have to connect with others. When you are more at ease, it is easier for your guests to feel at ease. When you model vulnerability, you make room for greater connection. When you are comfortable yourself, you create a cozy environment and your guests will feel comfortable too. When your heart is focused on the people in front of you and how you can best serve them, your hospitality personality will shine!

My hospitality personality has a lot to offer and so does yours. Be true to yourself. Don't fight against how you were created, but do adjust when required. Lean into your secondary hospitality personality when you need to balance out your weaknesses, or use those moments to let someone around you exercise their strength. When you do, you will be offering the best version of yourself: a relaxed host who is hosting within their hospitality personality.

Now that you know your hospitality personality, we are going to name your hospitality *habits* (why you host the way you do), learn how to navigate your hospitality *hurdles* (what stops you from wanting to host), and recognize what you can do to negotiate your hospitality *hang-ups* (what keeps you from enjoying hosting). After working through each of these areas, you will be able to effectively use your gifts of hospitality and extend love to others.

PART 2

your
hospitality
habits

We are what we repeatedly do. Excellence then,
is not a single act, but a habit.

Aristotle

CHAPTER THREE

setting

open home or closed home

Having identified your hospitality personality in chapter 2—Leader, Entertainer, Includer, or Organizer—now let's consider how your hospitality personality aligns with the five components of hosting: setting, scheduling, serving, socializing, and sharing. Each of these areas plays an important role within hospitality, and you likely already have habits established in each of them. Some of these habits may be because of your hospitality personality and others due to your life season. Within the four hospitality personalities, the range of habits will be individual and unique. There is not an exact formula. For example, one Leader may have differences in each of their habits compared to another Leader. While there are some tendencies within each of the personalities, your personal habits will align specifically to you and may continue to vacillate as you move through your different seasons of life. In other words, you and your hosting habits are unique to you, just like your hospitality personality!

By recognizing and naming your habits, you will have a clearer understanding of how to maximize your hosting opportunities.

It's easy to keep going through the motions of life without taking the time to examine how and why we do things the way we do. When you take a closer look at your intentional and unintentional hospitality habits, it will help you consider the different ways you'd like to grow as a host.

> It's easy to keep going through the motions of life without taking the time to examine how and why we do things the way we do.

The first habit, *setting*, refers to your current life setup and the atmospheres in which you like to host. I'm going to touch specifically on whether you need to have more of an "open home" or a "closed home."

There are reasons and seasons for both, and neither is better or worse than the other. When we hear the word *hospitality*, we tend to make two assumptions: one, that we host guests in our home, and two, that we serve food and beverages. While these two circumstances are often the case, they do not have to be the only way to host or extend hospitality.

Setting: Open Home

On a teeter-totter, with an open home on one end and a closed home on the other end, our suburban home, in this particular life season, mostly falls toward being an open home. I don't know if this was a deliberate choice we made, but it is something that both my husband, David, and I personify. We like to have people over. We enjoy having our kids' friends drop by unannounced. In fact, we've even become accustomed to kids just walking in through our front door without knocking or using the garage door code to let themselves in. Our house is rarely quiet, and for this season this has definitely become our new "normal." It probably goes without saying that our house has its fair share of clutter and chaos due to all this coming and going!

An open home means you like having people over, and therefore, you tend to have people in your home. You like initiating the invite, preparing your space, and gathering everyone together within your four walls or on your back patio. Whether you are single and living in a townhome, sharing an apartment with a roommate, empty-nesting in your forever home, or surviving in your two-story house with a bunch of rambunctious and messy kids—whatever your home or space looks like, you tend to lean toward having more of an open home. You do well with using your personal oasis as a way to serve and connect with others. You are available and willing to host—in your home.

If you are in a season of life when your home, health, and lifestyle are conducive to creating more of an open-home concept, capitalize on this reality. Use your location and your resources to open your doors and welcome others in. If, in your current season, you are able to use your abode as a blessing—and it is also a blessing to you—then do so!

This is us. Currently we have a home with extra space. We have a dedicated guest room and a great room floor plan that makes it really easy to entertain all different sizes of groups. We also have the time in our schedules to host with relative ease. I have flexibility with my work, as does David, and collectively we are mostly able to keep our house somewhat tidy, or at least we are able to do a quick reboot before guests arrive. Due to our calendar and commitments, if we want to have someone over for dinner, even on a whim, it usually doesn't require too much of an effort. We also try to not take ourselves too seriously. We're OK if our home looks lived-in and if everything is not in its place. We believe that this is one of the best ways to help our guests feel relaxed, and it also takes some of the pressure off of us. We want our guests to sense that we are more focused on connection than perfection. We want to be in the moment with our company, so we choose to let go of having everything "just so." And we tend to gravitate to people who do the same.

We've also modeled an open-home concept to our kids, so they're used to it. They too like having people over. We've had many a houseguest over the years. During our first year of living overseas, we had a stretch of almost six months straight where we had guests (family and friends) visit and stay with us! I remember sometimes having just enough turnaround time to get the sheets and towels washed and the beds remade. We loved and appreciated that our friends and family made the sacrifice, of both time and money, to come and visit us. These visits provided wonderful experiences and memories. Memories of family church in the living room, silly games played around the kitchen table, a roomful of people enjoying tasty appetizers and festive drinks, bike rides along the boardwalk, kids splashing in the pool, walks on the beach, and even an occasional dance party.

As a family, we value having people over and we like using our home to socialize. We've found that because we often open our home, hosting has become natural for all of us. It's become a habit.

However, it's important to mention that David usually wants to have people over more often than I do. He's an Entertainer through and through, and he gets energized by any and all social situations. This is the guy who was voted "King of Verbosity" in high school! Because I'm an Organizer, I don't typically share the same level of enthusiasm. I usually need more downtime (or time by myself) and generally associate hosting with the automatic need to plan and coordinate things. (Flying by the seat of my pants has never been my modus operandi.) Likewise, two of our kids tend to need more downtime too; they can't necessarily keep up with David's high level of hosting energy. The good news is that we have learned to balance how often we open our home and how to work together as a hosting team and family.

Whether you live with friends or family, consider each person in your home and their individual hospitality personality. When it comes to setting up more of an open home or a closed home, be sure to consider the individuals in your home first. An open home can be a blessing, but always make sure to care for those inside of your home before pivoting and taking care of those outside of your home. Respect individual needs, preferences, capacities, and capabilities. In doing so, you will create a stronger foundation for your hosting.

If your home is harmonious, then your hosting will feed off that energy.

If you live by yourself, then you get to decide this for yourself. The buck stops with you! That said, I would recommend asking a trusted family member or friend if they think you are doing too much or too little in this area. Seek honest feedback. Asking for counsel can be a helpful way to see some things that you may not be able to see for yourself. Your growth may be that you need to practice saying yes less often. Or vice versa. Being true to yourself in your current season of life is what's important.

Acknowledge your preferences and the setting that works the best for you as well as those you live with. I am not advocating that we should all have open homes or that you should have an open home all of the time. I want to encourage you to do what you need to do in this particular season. It could be that you need to have a 50/50 home right now, sometimes open and sometimes closed.

Setting: Closed Home

You don't *have* to host in your home! Hosting does not have to be where you live. You can gather people together just as easily at the local coffee shop, the park, a 5K run/walk, the bowling alley, or your favorite pizza restaurant. With certain people, picking a neutral location can be just the boundary you need to put in place in order to enjoy their company in a meaningful way. Meeting up somewhere other than your home can give you greater flexibility and allow you to leave if and when necessary.

It's often easier to host if you don't have to host in your house. Meeting up at a central location can take the pressure off of needing to clean, tidy, shop, and cook. A central location allows you to simply show up! Hosting pressures can be mitigated by creatively looking for different ways to gather. Do what you are able to and then rest in your best! Care for yourself first and you will be better equipped to care for and serve others.

Also, if you are in the middle of a trying or tiring season, then consider having a gatekeeper, a person who can help you with honoring the boundaries for your home and time. If you provide a point of contact and set up visiting hours, it can help you to still welcome people in but in a way that works best for you and your situation.

When our kids were younger, we were bound by different limitations, such as afternoon nap times and early bedtimes. (I sure do miss those early bedtimes!) In that season of life, we tended to host from time to time rather than on a regular basis. We needed more downtime because so much of our energy was being spent caring for our littles. Our schedule was dictated by different constraints and responsibilities, which meant that our priority to host was not ranked as highly as it is now—mainly because we didn't have as much time and/or energy available to host. Raising toddlers is tough!

There have also been life seasons when our schedules were fuller and our ability to host in our home was limited. Instead of fighting this reality, we worked to accept it. Some seasons just have more hustle and bustle than others. When this happens, the best thing you can do is consider having more of a closed home. A closed home doesn't mean that you never have people over; it just means that you may not do so as often.

Your home needs to be your safe place. Realize that if your tank is empty you won't have much to give to others anyway. Whether you prefer more of a closed home because of your hospitality personality, specific circumstances, or priorities in your current life season—you have permission to use the necessary boundaries.

If you are in a season with increased levels of stress, major life transition(s), health struggles, or some form of a crisis, then it might be wise for you, for now, to have more of a closed home. If you are in a position in which opening up your home is not a blessing but rather a stressing, then by all means give yourself the permission to host differently or maybe not at all. Perhaps you are finishing a degree, planning your daughter's wedding, nursing a newborn, caring for an aging parent, starting a new career, relocating across the country, dealing with a life-altering illness, or something else. If life is requiring all you have, consider having more of a closed home.

Your Habit: Open Home or Closed Home

"Hospitality isn't a contest. It is sharing the best *you* have."[1] "Sharing the best *you* have" is a refreshing way to think about hosting. If you love to have an open home but have gotten out of the habit of having people over, what steps can you take to initiate an invitation? What about hosting one dinner around your table this month? Or coordinating a TV night and having your friends over to watch the show with you? Or texting a friend to come over for a cup of coffee or tea?

Or, if you've fallen into the habit of always being the one to host and you want to start a new season with better boundaries at home, give yourself permission to take an event off or restructure things. You don't need to be the default host or always host in your home. You have the choice to make a change. You can create a new hosting habit.

The ultimate hope of hospitality is to build connection; feel free to define whether your home needs to be more of an open or closed home. Keeping an intentional mindset surrounding the atmosphere and setting of your hosting will help as you approach each month, holiday, and event.

Intentionally knowing what your home needs to be in your current season is important because hosting should also be a gift to you! You don't have to announce where you are with this habit, but you should be able to rest in your present reality. You may have more of a closed home with some people and an open home with others. You have different types of relationships, and the settings in which you host should align with how you interact within each of these relationships.

Give what you can today and do what you can tomorrow. Open or closed, it's up to you and the others in your home. Your habits around the setting can and should be continually shifting and changing, just like the seasons. Your home is your setting, and you get to set the boundaries for how, when, and where you host—with permission to redefine this habit in each and every life season.

What is your habit on the scale of setting? On the line below, mark an X where you are today. If you'd prefer to move from where you are now, mark a star where you'd like to be.

OPEN HOME   CLOSED HOME

CHAPTER FOUR

scheduling
planning or spontaneity

My youngest daughter, Berkley (an Entertainer), started her first day of seventh grade on the run. She left in the blink of an eye, dashing barefoot out the front door with her socks and shoes in one hand and her backpack in the other and yelling to me that she didn't have time to brush her teeth or take her first-day-of-school picture. Thankfully she made it to the bus on time and I did get that first-day-of-school photo—it just happened to be two weeks after the fact!

On the flip side is my son, Connor (an Organizer). For his first day back to school he had scheduled to get up earlier than normal, meticulously planned and coordinated his outfit, and color-coded the arrangement of his notebooks in his backpack. Due to his impeccable planning, we had more than enough time to take not one, but multiple pictures of his first day back to school. Connor tends to take after me just a wee bit.

Berkley did miss out on being able to take care of some of her essential responsibilities (like brushing her teeth!), but her spontaneous nature demonstrates that while she may not necessarily be as prepared as Connor, she still manages to make things happen. The striking difference between their two scheduling styles demonstrates that we're all shaped differently and our scheduling habits impact our day-to-day living.

Scheduling is an important component of hospitality, as it will often determine whether you end up creating the time to connect. As we discussed with regard to your setting, your scheduling habits too may ebb and flow. You may flow between wanting to plan or wanting to be spontaneous. This will likely depend on your hospitality personality and how you feel about the different events you are contemplating hosting or attending.

Thankfully, there is a place for both spontaneity and planning. The fundamental piece is knowing when to embrace which one!

Scheduling: Planning

I conducted a survey and asked my readers what they enjoy least about hosting. From their responses, one of the top three struggles was scheduling. The common themes were that it can be difficult to initiate an invite, challenging to find the time to plan, and most of all, hard to coordinate everyone's schedules because of how busy everyone is. I can relate to all of these feelings and experiences.

On more than one occasion I've been out running errands and bumped into a friend, someone who I may not have seen for several months. We reconnect, give each other mini life updates, and then one of us says something like, "We have to get together!" We finish chatting, don't schedule anything, part ways, and six more months pass before our next encounter or bump-in.

This happens because, as my readers shared, *everyone's schedules are busy*. I personally prefer to say that I have a "full" schedule, and I believe that we *should* have full schedules. Fullness means that we are going and doing. However, because of the fullness in our lives, if we want to foster increased connection we need to place some emphasis on the planning piece.

COMMITMENT-RELUCTANT CULTURE

Why can't we seem to commit? Sometimes everyone—me included—can be flaky and not respond or commit when invited to something. This can look like someone waiting until the last minute to respond, or initially saying yes and then changing their mind, or just remaining vague about whether they will attend. I think there are several reasons for this.

First, we have so many options for how we can choose to spend our time. If you want to catch a festival, a concert, a fun run, or a sporting event, there are usually more choices than there is time.

Second, we are living in more efficient times. It's easy to feel as though we can take on even more commitments simply because we are able to get more done in less time; in the end, though, we overcommit and have to cancel.

Third, we can feel as though we are connected with others because we are able to "check in" daily (or even hourly) and see pictures and snippets of each other's daily activities. This 24/7 swiping access can effectively decrease the urgency we might otherwise feel to connect face-to-face.

If you find yourself struggling to commit as a guest, I urge you to make a point to be thoughtful and timely with your response. It can be hard to initiate an invite; don't make it harder on the host by not committing one way or the other. It is always kind to respectfully respond and let someone know of your intentions, especially when they are trying to plan and prepare.

Hoping that things will happen doesn't usually work out as well as deliberately planning to make them happen! Hope alone is generally not a strategy.

Instead, when I run into a friend, it would be more intentional of me to schedule something on the spot. If we were to take advantage of the opportunity in the moment, then we would be able to get something on our calendars and not run the risk of letting time pass us by.

If you desire to be more intentional with your hospitality and are not in the habit of planning, consider the value it could play in your hosting. Start small and give yourself a goal. Create a list of who you'd like to schedule time with and then work down the list when you have an opportunity to offer an invitation. Or set up a hosting calendar to help you with your planning. Or reach out to one new person this week, even if just via text or email. *Connection of any kind can be a form of hospitality.*

I encourage you to be brave with extending invites! People love to be invited and they love to feel included. If they decline, don't take it personally and ask them again next time. Take the first step and extend love to those people God has put in your life. If you feel the prompting to reach out, then make the effort and don't hold back!

Use your planning skills to make hospitality a priority, but also remember to check in with your calendar and make sure you are not overscheduling. Be careful to not fall into the habit of having everything planned with no margin for spontaneity (I'm talking to you Organizers out there). Try leaving more room in your schedule so you can accept an invite from a more spontaneous friend (I'm saying hi to all you Entertainers!). Planning has its place, and spontaneity does too!

Scheduling: Spontaneity

I'm a planner. If you read my book *Take Back Your Time*, you already know this about me. I'm a calendar girl through and through.

Being more of a planner usually helps me to get things scheduled and make things happen. However, not everyone is a planner like me, and I've realized that it's important for me to also be able to adapt and flex when necessary.

Some of my favorite memories are from when things just happened. After a recent Saturday road trip to Boulder, Colorado (an hour from our home), to watch a soccer game, eat brunch, and do some shopping, I was happy to finally return home. I had transitioned into my comfy lounge clothes—basically elastic and cotton everything; my hair was in a messy bun on the top of my head; and I was most definitely settled in for the rest of the night. And yes, it was only three o'clock in the afternoon. It was at this point that David told me our friends had texted and invited us to come over and eat chili with them while they hosted their twelve-year-old daughter's birthday party. Part of me thought, *No, I'm comfy, I'm home, I'm settled.* Then the other part of me thought, *I love hanging out with them, it's a yes! Carpe diem!*

I laid down my planning preference of just staying home and opted for spontaneity instead. I wanted to live in the moment and connect with our friends. Our time spent over steaming bowls of chili and yummy birthday cheesecake was indeed worth it. Time with cherished friends always is. I'm thankful we had the time available to spend with them. My desire is to keep enough margin in my calendar that I can respond to spontaneous invites and also be able to extend them.

If you are *not* in the habit of being spontaneous, look for small ways to start being more impromptu with your scheduling. Maybe ask your neighbor to take a short walk when you have an extra thirty minutes, text a friend to see if they have time to grab a cup of coffee, or have a conversation with someone rather than moving right on to your next thing. These are all simple things that people can usually squeeze into their day.

Also, consider the places you go regularly—work, restaurants, school, gym, stores, church, and kids' events—and look for ways to be hospitable. Spontaneous hospitality with strangers may look like holding the door open, looking someone in the eyes, offering a kind smile, putting something back where it belongs, showing interest, or asking questions. In the Tyree house we often say, "It's better to be interested than interesting." It shows you care.

Showing others—those you know and those you don't know—that you want to connect, help, or serve them are all ways to express hospitality. It's the act of being present that demonstrates love.

> It's better to be interested than interesting.

One day when preparing to leave the gym, I was nearing the exit and saw that an elderly woman had just fallen down and was having a hard time getting back up. I watched as a kind young man offered her assistance. He helped her get back up and regain her footing, and then he guided her slowly to a nearby bench so she could sit and rest. As I watched this take place, I was touched by his gentleness, sensitivity, and most of all by his heart. He was modeling a heart of hospitality. He was compassionate and thoughtful. He was the perfect example of how to give spontaneous hospitality. One stranger serving another stranger. Hospitality in action!

Your Habit: Planning or Spontaneity

As with most habits, it's usually best to find balance and moderation. You don't necessarily want to feel like everything is scheduled down to the second or that there is no schedule at all. As you look more closely at how you plan your time, specifically when it comes to your hospitality efforts, consider where you need more planning and less spontaneity. Also examine where your schedule needs less planning and more spontaneity. My guess is that most of us need more balance.

A great example of using planning and spontaneity simultaneously is something my darling friends April and Abby, who are sisters and amazing cooks, shared with me (they also share a great hosting theme in chap. 17). They bring a gas fire pit out to their driveway and provide all sorts of s'mores and snacks. Then they invite their neighbors to share their food and fire. It's not necessarily scheduled, but it's planned and spontaneous all in one. It's low-key, a short time commitment, and maybe most importantly, easy to host! This is a fantastic way to show love to your neighbors and practice hospitality.

As you consider your scheduling habits, remember that it all comes down to having a balanced approach. If you hope to build more community and grow your hosting skills, then finding the sweet spot between planning and spontaneity is helpful. Often, we need to adjust things to better align with what we are hoping to do or experience. Setting goals and arranging how you will execute them is a great way to better realize your hopes for hosting. Generally, Leaders and Organizers will probably need to work on being more spontaneous, and Entertainers and Includers will probably need to work on planning more.

Let's be examples of never being too busy for people. Let's set our chairs out around the fire pit and invite others to come sit with us. Let's be the first ones to help pick someone up when they fall down. Let's practice presence. Whether planned or spontaneous, showing up is what usually counts the most.

What is your habit on the scale of scheduling? On the line below, mark an X where you are today. If you'd prefer to move from where you are now, mark a star where you'd like to be.

PLANNING   SPONTANEITY

CHAPTER FIVE

serving

foodie or non-foodie

Shauna Niequist's book *Bread & Wine* inspired me to want to cook more. When I was done drooling/reading through the pages, I decided to attempt making risotto using her recipe. Before reading *Bread & Wine*, my only experience with risotto had been having it a time or two at a restaurant. I'm happy to share that my attempt to try my luck with a new recipe turned out, and my creation of cheesy goodness was indeed delicious! I also now know where to find arborio rice in the grocery store. Thanks, Shauna!

If someone were to ask me to describe risotto, I would say it is a "cheesy rice dish." In contrast, Shauna describes it like this: "Risotto is my go-to entertaining meal. I like the process of it— toasting the arborio rice, the brash sizzle when the wine hits the pan. Risotto lets you know what's happening at every turn. Risotto-making is the exact opposite of baking, where it all happens in the oven without you. Risotto shouts out each step, invites you to notice each change. It's physical and active and clear. I like that about risotto."[1]

I've identified two camps when it comes to serving food (whether cooking or baking): those in the "foodie" camp and those in the "non-foodie" camp. Neither of these terms are negative; they simply describe how we as individuals tend to feel about food and the food experience.

Shauna (I'm guessing she's a foodie?) describes in artistic detail how to make risotto and expresses how she perceives the entire experience. She also considers this to be one of her go-to entertaining meals! Impressive. She pulled me into the cooking process, and I almost felt as though I was toasting the arborio rice alongside her. However, when I went to make my own risotto, I didn't hear any shouting from the risotto, and I didn't find the process very enlightening. It felt like I was making rice. I am more of a non-foodie.

From my reader survey, half of the respondents shared that they like to cook, and the other half said they do not like to cook. I think there are many different reasons for this, but some of it may be due to the reality that cooking isn't the daily necessity it once was. Restaurants are in abundance, and dining out or having takeout has become somewhat of a weekly or even daily activity for many of us. Meal-service companies and food-delivery offerings are now convenient alternatives that make it easier than ever to stay out of the kitchen. Nowadays you can have a sandwich delivered right to your front door by simply using an app on your phone.

The art of cooking is still alive and well, but the need to cook as an everyday activity just isn't what it used to be. While there is still generally a cost savings to cooking at home, our culture is also strapped for time, which has created an increased demand for food conveniences and services. Emmie Martin profiled some of the research on this trend in her 2017 article:

> In the *Harvard Business Review*, researcher Eddie Yoon shares data he's gathered over two decades working as a consultant for

consumer packaged goods companies. Early in Yoon's career, he conducted a survey that determined that Americans fell into one of three groups:

- 15 percent said they love to cook
- 50 percent said they hate to cook
- 35 percent are ambivalent about cooking

When Yoon conducted the same survey 15 years later, the percentages had changed. Only 10 percent of consumers professed a love of cooking, while 45 percent said they outright hated it and 45 percent were on the fence.[2]

So even though serving food and beverages is often a responsibility associated with hospitality, it's important to remember that this isn't a responsibility that is natural for everyone. For many, this may be an underdeveloped habit they have chosen to avoid altogether. Others don't make the time to cook or feel like they have the time. And while food is a common central theme of hospitality, it doesn't need to be the main emphasis or top priority.

Food should have a place, but only a place that works for the host.

Serving: Foodie

My sister Harmony is a foodie. She makes her own pasta, magically creates recipes, and definitely views cooking as a hobby. For her, cooking is relaxing and something to look forward to. It's a way to express herself and sometimes even a way to unwind at the end of a long day.

One summer, before meeting up for a visit in Italy, she emailed me and asked if I would like to attend an Italian cooking class with her when we would be together in Tuscany. It took me about two seconds to respond with a "No, thanks." While I truly appreciate the art of cooking and do enjoy watching other people work to master their craft, I just don't have the same desire to whisk, broil, mince, and simmer. I have had to develop into a cook of sorts (mainly because I have a family to feed), but cooking will never be something that I want to spend *more* time on. I'm all about Taco Tuesdays and Breakfast for Dinner, and a one-pot recipe is my best friend. Simple is my go-to theme, because for me, simplicity gets dinner done!

For Harmony, cooking is clearly something she is passionate about and a habit she discovered and developed at a young age. I remember being a teenager and watching her work tenaciously, up to thirty minutes or more, to perfectly craft a gourmet sandwich. Meanwhile I was just as happy to microwave a bag of popcorn and eat it straight out of the bag. She can't help but savor the experience of cooking. She serves her guests delectable meals and puts her heart into it. She's the one who taught me about king crab, mozzarella and tomato antipasti, and charcuterie boards. I love having dinner around her table.

If you, like my sister Harmony, find yourself in the foodie camp, then this hosting habit may feel relatively natural for you. In fact, you may enjoy this part so much that it's primarily why you host, and that's fantastic! (And yes, I'd love to come over for dinner—just please don't ask me to bring queso.)

Foodies, you are very much appreciated. You know how to turn food and dining into an experience. Those of us non-foodies are so thankful for you. Your ability to cook delicious foods is an excellent way for you to shower your guests with love. The only thing I want to caution you on is this: keep your guests the center and your food the sides. If you become overly focused on your menu and what you are serving, you may inadvertently create more pressure on yourself or your guests.

> Keep your guests the center and your food the sides.

Use your cooking to celebrate your guests and to serve them your best. Realize that some of your guests will appreciate your attention to the food and others might just be grateful that they didn't have to cook! Try to keep things simple and nonintimidating. This will help your guests feel more comfortable reciprocating the invitation, especially if they tend not to cook as elaborately. Food can be a focus of hospitality and a blessing to others. Food plus fellowship is a great recipe for community building.

Serving: Non-Foodie

My friend Ashley shared with me that on Thanksgiving she and her family prefer to hit the slopes on their snowboards and then stop by a buffet restaurant on the way home. This sounds wonderful to me. I mean, no shopping, no cooking, and best of all—no cleanup! For the foodies out there, your jaw probably just dropped to the floor! Thanksgiving *without* a home-cooked dinner?!? But it looks to me like Ashley is onto something. She gets her family to drive several hours up to the mountain, which provides built-in talk time—something that can be hard to experience when you have teenagers all going in different directions. They are able to connect as a family and build memories, all while winding up the roads and cutting down the slopes. I'm also thinking that the buffet dinner might be a favorite highlight for her two teens. Who needs a home-cooked turkey and mashed potatoes when there is all-you-can-eat chicken nuggets and frozen yogurt?

If you find yourself more in the camp of being a non-foodie, I have good news for you! You can still serve appetizing meals and have many options to help you with meal preparation.

If you plan to cook a meal, I suggest you stick with a tried-and-true recipe. Deciding to make a "new" recipe when hosting is usually not a good idea, unless maybe you are a foodie through and through. Foodies (often the Entertainers and Includers) can generally pull this off as they are usually the ones who can also create recipes off the cuff. Because of my kitchen skills, I tend to stick to either serving lasagna or enchiladas. These are two dishes that I can make without looking at the recipes. I've also made each of them countless times, so I know with almost a certainty that they will turn out and be a hit! Also, by serving these main entrees I know the side dishes that go along well with them and this gives me an automatic "theme" and menu plan. And it makes it easy for me to let my guests know what they can bring should they offer to bring something.

Or consider taking a 50/50 approach. Try organizing your menu so that half of the items can be homemade and the other half can be store-bought. For example, if you decide to go with an Italian theme, plan to make your spaghetti and salad. Then buy a loaf of freshly baked bread and some ice cream. By simplifying your menu and required prep time, you will decrease your workload by half, and who doesn't love ice cream?

A relaxed host knows when to be flexible! If cooking and serving is something that you don't have the time for or you don't have the interest in doing, consider catering the meal, picking up takeout, or meeting at a restaurant. Sometimes you may want to host and serve, and other times you may want to host and delegate the cooking to someone else. Choose to be flexible. You can keep a non-foodie habit and still practice gracious hospitality. From potlucks to BYO (bring your own) barbeques to sandwich and salad bars, there are so many ways to streamline the cooking and serving process. Remember the main purpose is to spend time together and to connect.

Also, don't underestimate your potential to be a better cook or baker. My mom (who's a great cook) has always said, "If you can read, you can cook." It just takes time and patience. Don't sell yourself short. If you want to become more confident in the kitchen, then by all means you can and should!

Your Habit: Foodie or Non-Foodie

I believe that food and traditional meals can hold a very special place in our hearts. While I was growing up, my family would always have a tortellini dinner with French bread and a cabbage salad for our Christmas Eve dinner. My mom had discovered that an easy-to-make meal was required after returning from either an evening church service or a holiday get-together. Which is why this is the dinner I've eaten every Christmas Eve for as long as I can remember, and I've also passed this tradition on to my kids. While the meal isn't anything fancy, it does hold memories and a special place in my heart.

If you are in the habit of being more of a foodie (often, but not always, Entertainers and Includers), then I'm guessing you probably don't have as many challenges when it comes to serving your guests. You, unlike me, probably have a beautiful set of steak knives and have most likely been successfully broiling bread since forever. It's likely not a struggle for you to plan a menu; instead it's more of a struggle for you to try and narrow down what you *will* prepare because you have so many favorites! As a foodie, you enjoy the process of cooking and you delight in serving your guests tasty and delicious meals. You definitely know what arborio rice is and where to find it in your grocery store.

If you are more of a non-foodie (often Leaders and Organizers), then the serving part of hosting can probably feel a bit more intimidating and unrewarding for you. Don't fret! I firmly believe that there is a place at the table for all of the foodies and all of the non-foodies. Wherever you fall on the scale—foodie, non-foodie, or anywhere in between—you have the ability to serve your guests well. Take a deep breath, use your strong leading and organizing skills, and never hesitate to delegate!

Keep your ultimate goal of hosting centered on the people gathered around your table. Make your habit of serving more focused on connection than on what you are serving. After all, we often remember the laughing and talking much more than we do the beverages or the food. Serve from your heart and keep flexibility your heartbeat. You can always develop more skills in the kitchen, and you can always simplify your menu to better serve your guests (and yourself). Keep in mind, no one finds a stressed-out cook a joy to be around.

Look for ways your hospitality personality can complement your cooking (or delegating), and most importantly, use your habits in the kitchen to help your guests feel relaxed and at home. Food is a way to connect, but it's only a tool. *How you use the tool is what's most important.*

I'm beginning to think we might hit the slopes for our next Thanksgiving. Dinner buffet here I come. I love frozen yogurt!

What is your habit on the scale of serving? On the line below, mark an X where you are today. If you'd prefer to move from where you are now, mark a star where you'd like to be.

FOODIE   NON-FOODIE

CHAPTER SIX

socializing

extrovert, introvert, or ambivert

Socializing can be complicated. Do you ever get an invite and immediately feel tired just thinking about having to respond or attend the event? Not because you don't like the idea of saying yes or because of the event itself (it may be an event that you think sounds fun). It's just that deep down, you feel conflicted. Or, are you more apt to receive an invite and not even think twice before saying yes? You hear the words "Let's get together!" and you are immediately all in? You love being invited and have a harder time saying no than you do saying yes. Deep down you are all about being with others; you have an attitude of the more the merrier! If you are a Leader or an Entertainer, you most likely lean more toward being extroverted and with an all-in attitude toward social situations. On the other hand, if you are an Includer or an Organizer, you might find that you lean more toward being introverted and can tend to vacillate between wanting to socialize and wanting to stay home.

As with each of the hosting habits, there is a sliding scale for socializing, and you likely fall somewhere between extroversion and introversion. There may be times you slide more one way or the other, depending on how you feel in the moment, where you are, who you are with, or what you are doing. When looking at the two styles (extroversion and introversion), you are considering what drains you and what fills you.

Here are some questions to consider as you think about how you prefer socializing. Reflect on these questions according to how you feel most often in social settings.

- Are you usually drained or filled after spending time with people?
- How do you like to recharge?
- Do you have lots of friends or a few close friends?

According to Kendra Cherry, 70 percent of us are ambiverts—falling somewhere in the middle of that sliding scale. "Ambiverts tend to enjoy both spending time with others and spending time alone, depending on the situation and their needs at the moment. Most importantly, remember that one type isn't 'better' than the other. Each tendency can have benefits and drawbacks depending on the situation."[1]

Where do you see yourself? Are you more of an introvert, an extrovert, or an ambivert?

The goal here is to understand your socializing habits, and as with each of the hosting habits, to play to your strengths. By playing to your strengths you

> By playing to your strengths you can be a more relaxed host or guest.

can be a more relaxed host or guest. Knowing who you are and why you do what you do is the first step! Then you can take the next step and use the specific guardrails you need to be able to best thrive in social settings. Your intention when it comes to socializing should be to make the necessary efforts to best set yourself up for success. Successful socializing looks like being at ease when you are with others. By setting yourself up for success you will be able to experience more positive interactions and memories.

Socializing: Extrovert

David is an Entertainer and is definitely an extrovert. One time at his Christmas work party, we were out on the dance floor, dancing away. I thought the idea was that we were to be dancing together (as a couple), but then when a new song came on (probably something by Michael Jackson), he switched gears and became "solo dancing guy." He began performing a break-dancing number as if he were sixteen again. I slowly backed off the dance floor and looked for a chair to collapse on. I could not keep up with his dancing style, nor did I want to be the center of attention. However, he loved the opportunity to be in the spotlight. In fact, he went out of his way to create the spotlight while I was quick to do the exact opposite!

During a marriage counseling session, we each took a test and scored high on opposite ends of the scale. He scored as being extroverted, and I scored on the other end as introverted. It was interesting to see this information on paper, because we had definitely sensed this tension in our relationship but we hadn't really been able to identify that this was the reason for it. We have since been able to work on better communicating and planning a more united approach when attending social events together.

For example, when we lived overseas, one expectation was for me to attend work-related dinners with David. After attending a few of these events, I had to have a sit-down with him and better articulate my needs. When we would go to an event, we would arrive and he would stay with me for a while, and then after a little bit he would float off and mingle like it was his job. Well, it was, but I needed him to also remain attentive to me. As an introvert, I'm not shy, per se, but I don't feel as comfortable mingling in large groups, especially when I don't know most of the people. These were his work parties; therefore, I usually knew only a few of the people attending. I found myself feeling somewhat socially awkward. For me, it was incredibly draining, and in the moment, I just wanted to retreat and head home.

We had to work through this predicament. David was getting energized and filled the more he moved around the room, but I was having the opposite experience. Our solution was that we would do more regular check-ins with each other. He committed to staying with me more and introducing me to more people. He also validated my feelings and realized that I was not as naturally comfortable as he was in those social settings. I didn't want to hold him back from who he is or who he needed to be, but I needed for us to remain on the same socializing team.

If you relate to being more of an extrovert, then you are most likely keen on spending lots of time in social settings. This doesn't necessarily mean that you have a high energy level, but it does mean that you love spending time with people. As a host or as a guest, you are usually energized by being in groups. Being with people charges you, and the time can often fly by! This is wonderful, but you'll want to make sure to keep in mind that not everyone has the same response to socializing. You want to be sensitive if your spouse, roommate, or best friend is on the other side of the spectrum. If so, it is vital that you work to respect and honor your differences. Note those times when you may need to slide more one way or the other on the socializing scale and also what you can do to help your plus-one be more comfortable in a social setting, especially if it's not their natural bent. Lastly, use your extroversion to help the introverts feel even more welcomed when socializing. Seek them out, ask questions, show interest. Ultimately, use your energy to bless others!

Socializing: Introvert

Being more of an introvert, I've realized that it's easier for me to be myself when I'm in a group ranging between two to eight people. In larger groups, I tend to pull back and not engage as much. If I'm at a table with ten or more people, I usually become more like a turtle and pull into my shell. I'm more inclined to sit back and listen to the stories and laugh at the jokes. I shift to becoming more of an observer than a participant.

What I've learned is that it's important for me to be true to the core of who I am. If I host a dinner party at my house, I most often prefer for it to be a smaller group. If I go to a girls' Bunco night, I am more likely to engage in one-on-one conversations than be the table storyteller. If I join a book club, I prefer that it be a smaller group because I know I'm more inclined to open up and discuss the book in that setting.

This doesn't mean that I won't go to large parties or that I won't take the opportunity to bust a move on the dance floor. It just means that I know myself and where I'm most comfortable. There are also those times when I slide toward being more of an ambivert, particularly within a group that I'm closely connected to. When this is the case, the size of the group becomes less important because I naturally feel more at ease due to the depth of the relationships.

The more I acknowledge how I socialize and how my habits affect my social experiences, the better I can prepare and be present. And when I'm prepared, I am more relaxed whether I'm hosting or attending.

If you are more of an introvert, you have a natural ability to connect well with people, especially one-on-one. Therefore, show your love and care for others by demonstrating interest and seeking conversation. You have much to offer; make a point to share who you are and seek out the other introverts! There may be times when you want to do things in a larger group and times when you crave a smaller group. Welcome both opportunities and do your best to enter each social setting fully charged and filled up. Knowing who you are will help you to not be as torn by whether to accept an invite or host.

Your Habit: Extrovert or Introvert

Knowing in which situations you slide more one way or the other on the socializing scale will help guide you as you plan gatherings, decide how to RSVP, and approach attending get-togethers. Understanding yourself and your habitual responses to social settings will allow you to more fully enjoy your time with others. When you consider which social settings align with your extroversion, introversion, or ambiversion habits (if you are somewhere between the two), you will be setting yourself up for increased blessing and more meaningful interactions. Accept and acknowledge where you fall on the socializing scale, and allow yourself to slide either direction as needed. Your ability to enjoy your social time will directly correlate with how well you match your habits to your choices. For you, this may mean busting out your best Michael Jackson routine on the dance floor, or floating between the larger and the smaller group, or needing to leave a party early just because you need to go home and get to bed.

Don't regret who you are or how social settings make you feel. You are hardwired this way, and you always have something to bring to the party no matter how extroverted or introverted you are. "Our lives are shaped as profoundly by personality as by gender or race. And the single most important aspect of personality—the 'north and south of temperament,' as one scientist puts it—is where we fall on the introvert-extrovert spectrum. Our place on this continuum influences our choice of friends and mates, and how we make conversation, resolve differences, and show love."[2]

Different social settings will tap into different parts of your energies. You may find that certain larger gatherings will drain you while others won't at all. You may not always feel the same way. Your energy will change depending on the differences between the settings of your social events. Allow for this reality and work to be relaxed within whatever energy you feel.

Make it your goal to set yourself up for hosting success by always considering what you need to have in place before and after a social get-together. Fill, drain, fill.

Extroverted? You will tend to feel most natural in the following social settings:

- where you can move around and engage with many different types of people
- where you can share stories, talk, and network
- where you can be of help to others

Introverted? You will tend to feel most natural in the following social settings:

- where you can connect with people on a closer, one-on-one level
- where you can listen and learn from others
- where you can help to facilitate things

What is your habit on the scale of socializing? On the line below, mark an X where you are today. If you'd prefer to move from where you are now, mark a star where you'd like to be.

EXTROVERT   AMBIVERT   INTROVERT

CHAPTER SEVEN

sharing

giving or receiving

Hospitality is a bridge that brings people together and helps build communities. It's not a one-sided experience. I think the most beautiful part of hospitality is that it centers on sharing. There is a giver and a receiver. The giver offers and the receiver accepts. Within this exchange, kindness and generosity are usually also a part of the equation.

My encouragement for you, as you examine your habits around sharing, is to consider how you can make efforts to be on both the giving side *and* the receiving side of hospitality. Falling into the habit of doing one more than the other isn't a good pattern to develop. When you are called to receive, accept the generosity. When you are called to give, give with gusto. Giving allows us to show our love to others and receiving allows us to let others demonstrate their love for us.

Like with the previous four habits, this habit also falls somewhere on a range between giving and receiving. There are times that you must step up and be a gracious giver and there are times when you must step down and be a willing receiver. There is a time and place for each. So let's see how you are doing with this habit!

Sharing: Giving

A great example of giving is what I like to call *secret hospitality*. This can happen in the drive-thru coffee line when someone pays for the drink of the person behind them. This is hospitality wrapped up in one small and simple gesture. Oftentimes after this event occurs, the gift keeps on giving. The receiver of the first gift then pays for the car behind them, and then that person pays for the person behind them, and it goes on and on, creating a hospitality chain reaction! I've heard of it happening up to thirty cars in a row.

One morning, when I was getting ready to drive to Denver, I decided to go through the Starbucks drive-thru and get a chai tea latte. When I went to pay, the barista told me that the car in front of me had already paid for my drink. I was shocked at this gesture of kindness and surprised because it had come out of the blue. I should have offered to buy the drink for the person behind me right then and there, but I didn't act fast enough. After that experience, I made a vow to never miss out on an opportunity to contribute to the gift of secret hospitality. I ended up following the car (of the person who bought my drink) for about thirty minutes south on I-25. This gave me more time to reflect on this person's kindness. I was deeply touched that this stranger had blessed me. It was unexpected and undeserved. I can still remember the warm feelings I felt that day; simple acts of giving can be far reaching.

As a family, we've made it a tradition to bless a server around the holidays. Last winter, we went out to eat at one of our favorite breakfast places on the morning of Christmas Eve. Before we went into the restaurant, we decided to leave a larger-than-normal tip for our server. We thought this was a great way to share generosity and also to recognize our server's hardworking efforts, especially on a holiday workday. It was so fun to see our kids get big smiles on their faces as we filled out the receipt and noted the tip amount. Then we left quickly, and while we wish we could have seen the reaction from the server, it was more fun for us to keep it a surprise. It's lovely to know that you can give something to someone unexpectedly and that they get to simply receive it.

When you heard the word *hospitality*, you might have automatically started to think about how you could show more kindness or how you might be able give to others more. This is wonderful! We are supposed to look for ways to serve others; God wants us to practice hospitality. We can be loving examples of Jesus here on earth. We can choose to take our eyes off ourselves and work to notice others more. We can use our hospitality gifts to reflect Jesus's love shining through us.

As you think about how you can give your gifts of hospitality, remember that hospitality can and should look many different ways. You don't have to host large dinner parties or open up your home. Sharing hospitality simply means sharing of yourself and being generous. Yes, you can be generous with your home or your cooking, but you can also be generous with your time, talent, energy, money, attitude, and so much more.

Use your hospitality personality and your sharing habits to give to those around you. Look for ways to stretch yourself, be creative, and extend yourself. Hospitality can be given to your loved ones but also to anyone God has put in your life. A warm greeting, a thankful tip, an unexpected compliment, or letting someone go in front of you—in traffic or in person—are all ways to demonstrate generosity. Just think: what would our streets and traffic patterns look like if we all practiced *more* hospitality while driving? Gasp!

> Look for ways to stretch yourself, be creative, and extend yourself.

You can also give by opening up your home, providing a meal for your neighbor, or setting up a social event to help gather people together. Giving can be defined by how you best and most naturally give. You do not have to give in ways that feel unnatural to you. When you honor this truth, your giving will feel more authentic and genuine and the receiver will be increasingly blessed.

How can you practice being a giver?

With your family/friends _____

_____

With your service/work _____

_____

With your life—home, church, neighbors _____

_____

Sharing: Receiving

After delivering my second child, my son, Connor, I was resting in my hospital bed when my friend Jamie showed up for a visit. As a young mom herself, she congratulated me and asked me all about the delivery. I, of course, quickly started to share with her (mom to mom) all about it. I had naively thought his birth would be similar to my first delivery—ha! After chatting and reconnecting, Jamie then offered to brush and braid my hair. I was touched by her offer and quickly said, "Sure!" (Although I have to admit that inside I was a little bit taken aback. Nobody had offered to brush my hair before, or at least not since I'd been a young child and needed help with brushing my hair.) I'll never forget Jamie's sweet offer. I sat there and humbly received her gift of care. As she gently and tenderly brushed my hair and fixed it into a French braid, a part of me felt vulnerable—I'm definitely more comfortable in my independence—but another part of me felt extremely loved. She was nurturing me at a time when I craved it. I was exhausted and overwhelmed, and battling all of the crazy post-pregnancy hormones and feelings. I chose to let down my guard and turned away from my bent toward independence. I graciously received Jamie's kind gift.

We must remember to make it a habit to allow others to be generous to us. We need to be open to receiving and gracious with accepting what others want to give to us. When we are, we're allowing others to offer their hospitality gifts to us and helping them shine in their hospitality personality.

I love what Katie Reid shared in *Made Like Martha* about her friend's experience. Her friend, Kris Camealy, wrote of a time when she chose to receive a generous offer.

> The other day I got an email from a woman I did not know, offering to bring dinner for my family. I thought about it, prayed about it, and wrestled with my fears over accepting her offer, because you know, #Strangerdanger. As I debated over what to do, I was reminded that hospitality isn't just about giving but also receiving— it's also about letting others give of themselves and be a blessing. And when this new friend showed up, with a bountiful box full of a complete dinner for the 6 of us? I was completely humbled. Her offering came because she is also attending #RefineRetreat [the event I host] and she imagined that in the midst of the last-minute details I'm working on, I could use a night off from cooking this week. She was right, and God knew I'd need her gracious generosity. If you're more comfortable giving than receiving, let me encourage you to accept the offers when you know you should. Let someone have the joy of blessing you.[1]

Isn't this a beautiful example of receiving generosity? It's an example of practicing being on the receiving end by allowing others to serve you and remaining humble in the process. While it is important to serve others, we must also allow room for others to serve us. If we only stay on the giving end then we are not providing others with the opportunity to bless us. Receiving is a great way to practice humility. It can mean admitting that you need help or that you need others in your life. (And we all do.)

Make it a habit to not only practice being a generous giver but also a gracious receiver. There is a time to remain independent and a time to shift toward dependence. Know when you need to accept a kind offer or when you need to allow others to step in and help you. You are not meant to do life alone. Your life is meant to be shared with others. When you allow others to give to you, you are opening the door for increased connection and community. You are trusting others with your needs.

How can you practice being more of a receiver?

With your family/friends _____

_____

With your service/work _____

_____

With your life—home, church, neighbors _____

_____

Your Habit: Giving or Receiving

There should be a natural tension between giving and receiving. You should not always be the giver nor should you always be the receiver. If you find that you gravitate toward being more of a natural giver (this can be more common for Includers and Organizers) or a natural receiver (this can be more common for Leaders and Entertainers), then consider where you need to make some adjustments. Giving or receiving may be practiced at home or work, with your family or friends, at the gym or at school. It can be developed and modeled in all areas of your life.

Share with the Lord's people who are in need. Practice hospitality. (Rom. 12:13)

Sharing requires that you give and that you also receive. Usually the foundational piece of this experience is that it will require you to use your time. Take advantage of your time when you are out and about, and look for opportunities to give to others. There are small ways to be hospitable everywhere you look! Likewise, if someone holds the door for you or offers for you to go in front of them at the grocery store checkout line because you have fewer items, accept the gift and thank them for their generosity. Whether you're giving or receiving, practice your hospitality by practicing humility. Help to build hospitable bridges in all of your communities, and keep an eye out for ways to offer secret hospitality too!

What is your habit on the scale of sharing? On the line below, mark an X where you are today. If you'd prefer to move from where you are now, mark a star where you'd like to be.

RECEIVING _____ GIVING

PART 3

your hospitality hurdles

Hospitality is simply love on the loose.

Joan D. Chittister

CHAPTER EIGHT

who

circles

In high school, I ran track. You know which event never tempted me in the least? The hurdles. Why would anyone want to jump over large obstacles time and time again, not to mention, as fast as possible? Not me. I'm a safety girl at heart. Daredevil is not, and never will be, my middle name. Instead I opted to run the long-distance events. I knew that by choosing them, my only hurdle might be having my shoelaces come untied during the race.

While I was able to dodge running the hurdles on the track team, I've realized I can't as easily escape the hurdles that come along with hosting. No matter your hospitality personality, there are hurdles as a host that you must learn how to jump over. And not with the same speed as on the track, but instead with discernment and sensitivity: sensitivity to yourself (and your hospitality personality) and discernment regarding who you will choose to share your hospitality gifts with.

As with your hosting habits, there are not set rules stating that if you have a particular hospitality personality then you will always have this hurdle and not that one. Your hosting hurdles are specific to you and your experiences. We all have hurdles, they are just different sizes and distances apart. However, depending on your hospitality personality, some of them may be easier for you to clear than others.

The five hosting hurdles are the five parts of an invitation: the who, what, where, when, and why. We all have some hindrances when it comes to hosting, and unfortunately, we can't just avoid them by electing to run a different event. Wouldn't that be nice?

These five hurdles all play a role in hosting, whether we like it or not. Nevertheless, you can more seamlessly navigate them by remembering your hospitality personality and your hosting habits. Use this information as a reference point for how you most naturally host or aspire to host. If you focus on your strengths and priorities, you will be able to more confidently get up and over each of your hosting hurdles. Are you ready? On your mark, get set, go!

Your Circles of Influence

My friend Julie Davis is the epitome of southern hospitality. I first met Julie the night of David's Christmas work party—which also happened to be the same night I was searching for a chair so I could graciously (or embarrassingly) exit the dance floor. The chair I happened to eventually find was at Julie and her husband's table. We only chatted briefly that night, but soon after we all became close friends. Our five years in Albuquerque are laced with memories of spending time with the Davis family. We learned not only how to embrace living away from our families but also how to welcome the new additions to our growing families.

Julie was born and raised in the South, and I was born and raised in the Pacific Northwest. Having grown up on the West Coast, I had never really been exposed to the southern way of living (or what I like to refer to as southern hospitality). When I would arrive at Julie's house, she would always offer me something to drink. She would say in her darling southern accent, "Can I get you something to drink?" She usually had sweet tea available, so I always answered, "Yes, please!" Her example of offering me a beverage (almost immediately) when I entered her home has always stuck with me. Her gracious offer communicated to me that she was also warmly welcoming me into her home. She was asking me to come in and *make myself at home*. She wanted to spend time with me. (By the way, this is my number one hosting tip: Always offer your guest something to drink and give them options—this provides an invitation for them to settle in and also gives them something to hold on to, which can help them to feel more at ease.)

Julie has taught me much over the years. Everything from how to make sweet tea to how to create fabulous Halloween costumes to how to trust Jesus with your whole life. One lesson she passed on to me that resonated with me in so many ways is the concept of your "circle." Julie explained to me that your (inner) circle is reserved for those who you are in closest relationship with. She described your circle as the people who have your back, who want the best for you, and who are there for you through thick and thin. Your circle may be your family members and those you consider to be your closest friends. Within your inner circle are your loved ones, those who you automatically want to call when you have good news, and maybe even more importantly, when you have bad news. They are your lifelines, your phone-a-friends, your cheer-leaders, your people, your team, your tribe.

As you look to who you want to extend hospitality to, start from the perspective of considering your different circles of relation-ships. You have an inner circle, your closest people. A middle circle, your acquaintances and your casual friends. And an outer circle, the strangers or people you know as a result more of circumstances than connection. Ideally you should be offering hospitality to each one of your circles. These are your *circles of influence*.

The hospitality hurdles come through learning how to best han-dle the different expectations and demands that are often placed on you. Within each of your circles you may sense different requirements and will likely have different approaches and specific boundaries you choose to implement. You must protect your own health first, because a healthy host is better able to give healthy hospitality.

Inner Circle—Family and Friends

In your inner circle you have your closest loved ones. In this circle, you may already have some automatic hospitality built in. For example, you may have a rotating schedule where you host two holidays a year for your extended family, or travel on an annual basis to visit your parents and/or siblings, or have a summer girls' trip that you never miss. In some ways, within your inner circle you may not have to be as intentional when it comes to extending invitations. There may be some default hosting and visiting already naturally in place.

CIRCLES OF INFLUENCE

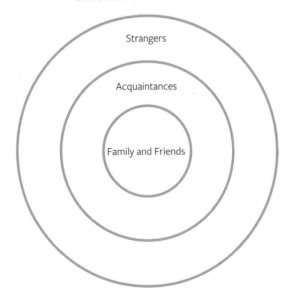

Strangers

Acquaintances

Family and Friends

However, sometimes these hurdles can be the most challenging to rise above because there may be times when the invitations (either way) feel more like expectation than connection. There may be pressure to gather just because you are related, or just because you live close by, or just because you have always done so in the past. Expectations can often inhibit potential intimacy.

In order to evaluate the health of your hosting (and your attending) with those you consider to be in your inner circle, take a step back and ask if there are obligations being communicated to you either verbally or nonverbally. Is there an undercurrent that feels more like pressure? If there is, then you may not be hosting or attending for the right reason(s). Also ask yourself if you are devoting the time to those in your inner circle that you want to. Are you giving the amount of attention to those relationships that you want to give? Are you investing well with those who are in your inner circle?

If your hospitality personality is an Includer or an Organizer, you may find it more challenging to put your foot down when you don't feel like hosting or when you don't want to attend something. It is important for you to recognize this about yourself (if you have this tendency) and not let others' demands rule your hospitality choices. While you can never control someone else, *you always have the ability to practice self-control.* If you are a Leader, you may find that you fall into the tendency of being more focused on your to-do list or your personal priorities than on carving out enough time to connect with the people closest to you. If you are an Entertainer, you may find that you intend to connect more with others but don't get around to it for one reason or another.

Be intentional about making your inner circle a top priority, specifically when it comes to your hospitality. This is your tribe; love them well. It is sometimes easy for us to give the worst of ourselves to those we are closest with. I know firsthand that my kids and my husband don't get enough of the polite and gentle Morgan that is more often seen out in public. Private Morgan has a harder time managing her manners. I'm more apt to lose my cool, snap demands, or be overly sarcastic just because these people are my family and I know that they love and accept me. I'm working to share more of my hospitality efforts at home with them.

Also, be discerning with who you allow in your inner circle. This is the circle of people who you will choose to be the most authentic, real, and vulnerable with. When you want to host an intimate gathering, this is who you choose to invite. When you need to make a guest list for a small dinner party or want to celebrate a major milestone or desire to plan a weekend getaway, this is the "who" you ask to join you. Your inner circle will likely ebb and flow as life goes on—as you move from place to place, change from job to job, or shift from life season to life season. The critical piece is knowing who is in your inner circle and protecting your inner circle. You have a limited amount of both energy and time available. Therefore, be discerning and intentional with who you invite to join you in your inner circle. It's vital that you have a healthy inner circle, a circle of people who are behind you. A friendship circle that is built on a foundation of support and understanding rather than expectation or obligation. Ultimately, this circle should be a source of filling for you, and there should be a healthy balance of both giving and receiving.

Middle Circle—Acquaintances

When we lived in Portland, Oregon, I had a lovely neighbor who would energetically wave and flash a beautiful smile whenever she drove by our house. I was usually either chasing toddlers or attempting to pull weeds, but every single time she rolled by, she made me feel known and noticed. It was a simple gesture, one that didn't cost her any time or money, yet it was a wonderful gift to me. We were just acquaintances and never hung out socially, but I felt connected to her. I knew that if I ever needed her for something, there was a good chance she would be there for me.

She showed me with her regular and consistent interactions that she cared about me.

Your middle circle is your catchall circle. This is where your acquaintances and casual friends hang out—varying from someone you hardly chat with at work, to your mail person, to your child's teacher. These are people you share some slice of your life with, yet you may not have as much direct or daily interaction with them. The beauty is that you still have a great opportunity to share hospitality with each and every one of your acquaintances.

When you choose to invite an acquaintance or someone you don't know very well to do something with you or to connect in some way, you may find that this person shifts from being in your middle circle to your inner circle. The compounded result of spending more time together may very well increase your level of friendship too!

The fantastic part of gifting hospitality to your acquaintances or casual friends is that it can often be done simply and naturally. Is there a coworker you could ask to lunch? Is there a neighbor you have never introduced yourself to? Is there a parent on your child's sports team that you've never really gotten to know? Is there someone you pass almost daily and still don't know their name? Is there someone you consider to be more of a casual friend but you'd like to become closer with? Think of all the natural times you have available to connect more with people. There are opportunities all around you!

What about bringing extra snacks to the sidelines and offering them to the other parents? Or picking up an unexpected cup of coffee for your boss? Or taking in your neighbor's trash cans? Or picking up a shift to help out a coworker? Or shoveling the snow off your neighbor's driveway (and keeping it a surprise)?

One easy way to share hospitality is to know and use people's names. People like to hear their names; it helps them to feel noticed. When you use someone's name, you demonstrate that you recognize them, you know them— just like my neighbor did when she waved and smiled at me. Recognizing others is a way to make them feel welcomed and loved. If you are less inclined to want to have others over to your home or in your personal space (if you are more introverted or are an Organizer or Includer), remember that welcoming others into any space is a way to offer hospitality. Being attentive and aware is hospitality.

Keep your eyes open and be on the lookout for those who are in your middle circle and who you might be able to reach out to even more. Your hosting should be an extension of grace and service. Ask God to help guide you in knowing who you should be extending more of your hospitality gifts to. He knows best who most needs your attention. Listen for his prompting, and most importantly, follow through. And always make a point, as you drive by your neighbor's house, to wave and smile!

> **Being attentive and aware is hospitality.**

Outer Circle—Strangers

In your outer circle are the people you don't necessarily know but do have some form of contact with. Strangers may be whoever you cross paths with, and hospitality toward them can take several different forms. It could be letting a car merge into traffic in front of you, offering a warm greeting to your server, or going out of your way to meet the newest coworker in your office even though you won't be working or interacting with them directly. We all want to be known, and sharing hospitality, even with those we don't really know, can be an incredible gift.

My daughter Ainsley recently had her car break down not once but twice in one week. The first time it happened, she called us in a panic because she couldn't get her car to start and she was stuck at a left-turn traffic light. We got there as quickly as we could, but as we pulled up to help rescue her, two gentlemen were already helping to push her car through the busy intersection.

The second time it happened (Did I mention it was in the same week?) she was a bit farther from home, and once again her stalled car was holding up traffic at a crowded intersection. A kind gentleman happened to witness the event out of his apartment window and promptly came out to help. He stopped what he was doing and swept in to help her in her time of need. He pushed her car to safety, offered to stay with her, and even asked if she needed more help. What a gift! He gave hospitality to a stranger, and his simple act spoke volumes.

> Do not forget to show hospitality to strangers, for by so doing some people have shown hospitality to angels without knowing it. (Heb. 13:2)

Sharing hospitality with a stranger is such a lovely thing to do. And yes, it usually isn't very convenient, as most hurdles aren't. The men who helped my daughter were most likely inconvenienced in some way. Loving others isn't always convenient. In fact, I might suggest that it's usually *not* convenient. It more often than not involves some form of sacrifice, and that's why it's a gift.

My challenge for you is to love and serve those in your outer circle. Look for ways to use your time, energies, and abilities. These people are also within your circle of influence, so look for opportunities to serve them too!

Your Hurdle: Who

Look for ways to offer hospitality to each of your circles in the ways that most closely align with your hospitality personality. Depending on your hospitality personality, you may find that sharing hospitality with some of your circles is more natural than others, and that is more than OK. The important piece to remember is that you can share equally yet independently. There may be times when you are able to give more to one circle than another, or times you have to reevaluate your boundaries or choices.

- For a Leader, it may be a hurdle for you to slow down and see your hospitality opportunities.
- For an Entertainer, it may be a hurdle for you to remain attentive to who needs something from you and what that is.
- For an Includer, it may be a hurdle for you to not over-extend yourself.
- For an Organizer, it may be a hurdle for you to initiate the invite.

I love how Reese Witherspoon's grandmother Dorothea describes hospitality: "Dorothea always said that . . . our famous hospitality isn't martyrdom; it's modeling. True southern women treat everyone the way we want to be treated: with grace and respect—no matter where they come from or how different from you they may be. Dorothea taught me to never abide cruelty or injustice. The Golden Rule, she said, applies to everyone."[1]

Hospitality is the Golden Rule in action: "So in everything, do to others what you would have them do to you, for this sums up the Law and the Prophets" (Matt. 7:12).

You have a hospitality race to run. So tie your shoes, select your event, and let the hurdle of "who" not be intimidating but inspiring!

Consider who you want to extend more hospitality to in each one of your circles. List those people here:

Inner Circle—Family and Friends

Middle Circle—Acquaintances _____

_____

Outer Circle—Strangers _____

_____

CHAPTER NINE

what

experience

For several years, David and I led a small group at our church, a group designed for parents with young kids. One of my favorite studies was *Parental Guidance Required* by Andy Stanley. Andy shared that we (as parents) tend to dial up the experiences for our kids and then consequently dial down our relationships with them. We can (maybe without even realizing it) put more emphasis on vacations, birthday parties, extracurricular activities, and academics than we do on building a depth of relationship with our children. I think there is a lot of truth to what Andy shared. It's tempting for us to try to do things bigger and better—maybe sometimes to keep up with the Joneses. We can forget to slow down and savor the people who are right in front of us. In our fast-paced, overindulgent culture it can be all too easy to put more energy into creating an experience than working on a relationship. This is not to say that we aren't spending time connecting with our loved ones, but rather that we are sometimes more focused on what something looks like than on what it truly is.

As you prepare to leap over your next hosting hurdle, the "what" or experience, you will be asking yourself questions like these: *What will my guests enjoy? What should the theme or focus be? What type of experience will work best for me and my guests?*

The *what* isn't always crystal clear; often there is a lot of leeway. What is freeing is that you as the host usually get to decide. I recommend that when you think about the type of experience you'd like to host, consider things from both your guest's perspective and your own. A harmony between both parties is a hosting win-win! Remember first and foremost that what is most important is that the experience be conducive to creating connection.

Guests

While living overseas, we had many guests visit us. Because they were traveling such long distances, they usually planned to stay with us for at least a few days and sometimes a week or more. One thing I learned from having so many houseguests is that each guest is unique. (Yes, they too each have their own hospitality personality!)

Some of our guests would arrive and hit the ground running. They wanted to see every piece of Portugal they could. They wanted to try *all* the restaurants, taste *all* the Portuguese wines, and walk along *all* the long stretches of beaches. They would get up early and stay up late, trying to maximize every minute of their time. They wanted to experience it all! Other guests would arrive and slowly ease into their vacation time. They would sit by our pool, take leisurely afternoon walks to the grocery store, and sleep in. They often liked lounging in the comfort of our cool living room, either reading or chatting. They would do some exploring but seemed to appreciate just as much being able to slow down and catch up on their rest.

One young couple visited us for a week, and I thought for sure that they would be up for all kinds of adventuring and touring. I assumed they would want to go, see, and do. Well, here's what I remember from their time with us. One afternoon while making dinner, I overheard them in the pool playing Marco Polo with my kids. Then another day the two of them were sprawled out in our living room laughing together and watching a TV show. It surprised me, but I also realized that this was probably exactly what they needed from their visit. And I was glad that we could provide that for them. We were able to offer them a comfortable and relaxing space to unwind and feel at home. They didn't conquer seeing all of the sights but met their more important need for relaxation and restoration.

We never really knew what our different guests' expectations might be until they arrived. We would try to have a conversation beforehand, but we also realized that with jet lag, culture shock, and the reality of shifting into "vacation mode," not all guests could accurately know ahead of time what they would need from us as hosts. They usually seemed to know better once they were with us and settled in. We learned to be flexible and let our guests experience what they needed to from their visit. We wanted them to get from their vacation what they were hoping to receive.

Whether hosting a short event or a long visit, consider what types of experiences might be the most meaningful to your guests. In better knowing your guests, you will better know how to plan.

For example, if your best friend is turning thirty and hates surprise parties, don't plan a surprise party for her! If your husband has always wanted a huge retirement party, see if you can find a way to make that possible. If your in-laws enjoy playing board games, then invite them over for a Friday game night. If your four-year-old son doesn't do well in large groups, then opt to plan a smaller-sized birthday party for him. If your neighbors are early birds, invite them over for brunch.

Thinking about what your guest(s) will appreciate and enjoy most will help you to set things up for success. They will feel honored if you have carefully considered their personal needs. Asking about everything from food allergies to preferences to various activity options are all thoughtful ways to show you care about what they like and don't like. You will be communicating that you want to know more about them and also help to meet their personal needs (as best you can). You can better tailor the experience when you know what they will appreciate the most. However, by no means do you need to cater to every wish or desire.

Host

As the host, you have a very important role. Regardless of your hospitality personality, you are in charge of leading the event. After acknowledging what will be the most meaningful to your guests, then consider too how you can orchestrate things so they are most meaningful (and manageable) for you.

One of the best ways to manage any hosting experience is to put an emphasis on simplicity and connection. Hosting doesn't have to be extravagant or ostentatious. In fact, I think it's often better (and more fun) when it's not. When you as a host acknowledge your hospitality personality and allow your natural hosting habits to assist with your planning, you will be modeling to your guests that you are more concerned with spending time together than with pulling off an event that has zapped all of your steam. By making things simpler, you will likely enjoy your hosting time more, and feel more relaxed too! This will also help your guests feel more comfortable and more inclined to offer a return invite. If you model an experience that is laced with grace, you will be emphasizing a tone of comfort and warmth.

> Model an experience that is laced with grace.

When you think about what kind of experience (party, occasion, celebration, gathering, event) you want to plan, always keep

97

a priority of making things simple. Simple doesn't mean boring. Instead it communicates "doable." Give yourself permission to delegate anything and everything you can, and especially those things that don't fall under your hospitality personality.

Work to uncomplicate things by knowing your limits, acknowledging your habits, and recognizing your strengths. If you take the focus off of creating an over-the-top experience and instead organize and plan a manageable (or doable) event, it will help you and your guests to have a better experience.

You can decide what "simple" means to you. Simple may look different to you than it does to me. As an Organizer, I might try asking for more help, especially if I feel that my time and schedule are already stretched too thin. If you are an Includer, you could choose to let go of some of the layers of details in order to streamline things. If you are an Entertainer, you could try to make some of the foods ahead of time or ask your guests to each bring a dish to share. If you are a Leader, consider leading the charge and asking your friends if they want to meet up at a restaurant for either appetizers or dinner. This way you'll avoid having to spend time grocery shopping, tidying, and cooking.

Your Hurdle: What

What you choose to do when you host is your choice. You as the host get to plan your party. Don't feel as though you need to set up an experience that doesn't match with your hospitality personality, and also don't feel as though you need to do things exactly as your guest wants them done. Your goal is to look for a balance. If both sides, the guest and the host, feel heard and understood, balance has probably been achieved. The event will be what brings you together and the time will be what provides you with the opportunity to connect.

To nurture and deepen relationships, we need both quality and quantity time. Generally, people prefer openness and closeness

A SURPRISE GIFT

One of my all-time favorite memories of a hosting experience was when we invited our friends and their baby over for a casual dinner. When they arrived at our house they stayed in their car for a while before coming to the door, and at the time we weren't sure why. We enjoyed a nice meal together. Chatted, laughed, and caught up, like you do around the dinner table. Then, when we went to the door to say our goodbyes, they asked if they could pray for our family. We said yes. We all reached out to hold each other's hands and made a circle in our entryway, and they prayed for us right then and there. What a gift!

My husband later asked his friend why they had stayed in their car for a while before coming up to our door that night. He replied that they were praying for us before they came in, something they like to do whenever they go over to someone's home. Again, what a gift! They were our guests and they gave US a beautiful experience. They chose to add to our time together (the experience) in such a rich and purposeful way. As a guest, you too can add to the experience in a meaningful way.

over pretentiousness and showiness. It's usually better to let your hosting center around a real experience than an ideal experience.

When leaping over the hosting hurdle of "what," work to dial down the emphasis on the experience and instead dial up the emphasis on the relationship.

And of course, simplify, simplify, simplify.

Jot down some experiences (parties, occasions, celebrations, gatherings, events) where you've either been a guest or a host, and indicate what you liked and/or didn't like about them. What are your takeaways about your preferences when it comes to the type of experiences that you like most or least? Use this as your own frame of reference as you move forward and plan to host.

_____

_____

_____

_____

_____

_____

CHAPTER TEN

where

venue

One day, when picking up something from the dry cleaner, I entered into a conversation with the woman working at the front desk. It was shortly after Thanksgiving, and the two of us landed on the topic of hosting houseguests. She told me that a friend of hers had to inform her guests that they couldn't bring their dogs along with them for their holiday visit (and stay in her home with them). It sounded like the guests had multiple dogs and felt it appropriate to bring them along. I'm unsure if this was a longer stay or if this was outside the normal. I didn't get all of the specifics. I also realize that in many situations and circles this is perfectly acceptable. However, from what I was told, this hostess didn't want to have the added houseguests (or sets of paws) over for the Thanksgiving holiday weekend. I find this completely understandable because it is her home and her space, and therefore, she is able to have her own set of house rules!

When navigating how to get over the hosting hurdle of "where" you plan to host, it is common to think that you should host in your home. This is sometimes the case, but it doesn't always have to be the case. There are obvious times, such as when you are hosting a wedding or a large party, that you might automatically look for an outside option rather than your home. But at many other times our homes are the first choice we consider. My suggestion is for you to begin at the starting line with this hosting hurdle and ask yourself a few questions before preparing to host:

- Which venue will be the best fit for the experience I want to facilitate?
- Which location will be the most accommodating (for me and my guests) and also coincide with the amount of time and energy I have available?
- Which venue will help me to most easily get to the finish line?

Reflect back on whether your current life season offers more of an open home or a closed home, as this too is an important factor.

Inside

Years ago, when we lived in Albuquerque, we started a tradition with our friends the Shields. We all loved the show *Survivor* so much that we decided to rotate houses on Thursday nights so we could watch the show together. Whoever's turn it was to host would serve dinner and dessert. It was a midweek treat that provided us with the opportunity to catch up with each other, enjoy a tasty meal, and discuss the highlights of the show. Hosting was relatively easy as there weren't big expectations when it came to the menu, ambiance, or activity. We would usually prepare an everyday menu, something like a big pot of soup or an easy-to-make casserole. We would settle into the living room, eat off of the plates that were balanced on our laps, and help ourselves when we wanted more. It was also a relatively short time frame because the show lasted only an hour and we usually had work to get to early the next day!

I really enjoyed hosting these *Survivor* nights. I would plan ahead, trying to think of something fun to make for dinner and dessert, and hosting the Shields family felt comfortable and natural. Even though we lived in a small, outdated home with carpet that badly needed to be replaced, it didn't matter. There were no expectations of being fancy, just fun. And fun we had. We kept the weeknight get-togethers going for a couple of years before we all had to part ways and move to different states.

However, when we relocated and moved back to our home state of Oregon, we discovered that our new neighbors, the Reveleys, also loved the show *Survivor*. So guess what? We resumed our Thursday night tradition! Only this time it looked a little different. We still rotated houses week to week but usually served less—often it was only dessert. We were in a new life season, now with three young kids, and the Reveleys had two school-age kids with various weeknight activities, such as sporting or school events. A favorite memory of our *Survivor* get-togethers was the night we walked around the corner to their house and they had tiki lights lining their walkway for the finale. It's the little things, isn't it?

These traditions are ones I hold on to dearly. We built memories week after week, and we really got to know one another. Tami (Shields) taught me all about scrapbooking and how to decorate beautiful cakes. Bonnie (Reveley) shared with me all about home-schooling and also modeled beautifully how to balance working and parenting. All of these connections were produced because we chose to gather together and watch a silly TV show!

If you decide to host inside your home, whatever the event may be, look for how you can best build in simplicity (like we talked about in the previous chapter). Plan a gathering that will feel manageable and enjoyable to you as the host. Acknowledge what will help you feel the most relaxed when you go to open your front door and greet your guests.

Welcoming someone into your home is a gracious gift. You are allowing them to enter into your world. This is something that should not be taken for granted by the receiver. In deciding if you want to host something inside your home, try making a mental list of the pros and cons. Ask yourself what will be the best "fit." Sometimes the best fit may be to open up your door and let others in, and other times it may not be. Hosting *Survivor* nights was a natural fit for me. We kept them casual, and I didn't feel any pressure to have our house look a certain way or to cook an elaborate meal. The nights were designed around connection, not presentation. The show, food, and drinks were all extras. It fit well to host these gatherings in our home, and I was always filled up after our time together. Hosting inside our home for our *Survivor* viewing parties felt almost effortless.

> Welcoming someone into your home is a gracious gift. You are allowing them to enter into your world.

When you decide to host inside your home, practice the art of letting go. If you can let go of your need to make things look perfect or to have all your ducks in a row, you'll be able to feel more at ease.

I love what Jessica N. Turner shared in *The Fringe Hours*. Jessica was expecting her friend for a visit. She wrote, "I was so nervous about her coming to my house. Would she notice that the mantel hadn't been dusted in a few weeks? Would the piles sitting on our desk make her think less of me? In the end, I just had to let it go and not worry about the state of my home. She knew I was on a book deadline, and she wasn't coming to see my house—she was coming to see me. Relationships are the currency that matters, not the condition of our homes."[1]

Amen.

Of course, you can consider the condition of your home, but what's so much *more* important is to consider the condition of your heart. If your desire is to spend time with people and to serve them, this may sometimes happen inside your home and sometimes outside of it.

There are times for both. Give yourself the freedom and permission to pick the right choice for you for each event. After all, either choice will get you to the finish line.

Outside

One year I decided to splurge and pay for a birthday party for my kids at one of those bouncy play places. I was practical (or cheap) and actually combined the party for my two oldest kids because their birthdays are only a month apart. While this option was a bit beyond our normal birthday party budget amount, I felt it was worth it because of the time and stress savings. And let me tell you—it was!

I had a short meeting with the coordinator, signed some forms, paid the fee, and was handed some blank invitations. Then, all I had to do was fill out the invites, send them to the guests, and bring the cake and party favors. That was it! It was such a simple way to host a party, and because I knocked out two of our kids' parties at once, it actually ended up being fairly economical too!

If you are strapped for time, feel that your house doesn't work well for hosting, or find that you tend to get overly stressed when hosting in your home, then why not host at an outside venue? Coordinating everything is often one of the biggest parts of hosting, and it can be made much smaller by choosing to host at an outside location. Outside venues typically mean less prep work and often less planning too.

A venue can be anywhere. Just go to your local Starbucks. So many of the patrons there are really just using the coffee shop as a place to gather. Starbucks is their venue. And it's not really costing them much (other than their beverage or food purchase). There is also no cleanup or setup, and it's easier to end a get-together when necessary because you are at a neutral location.

Neutral locations can be very beneficial, especially if you need to emphasize certain boundaries. You don't have to ask someone to leave if it's getting too late or your roommate is sick. Instead you can just get up and leave! While this may not be a common challenge, it sometimes can be. If you or your guests have varying time preferences or schedules, a neutral location can better mitigate all of those differences.

We learned from experience that in the Portuguese culture, arriving to a social event thirty or even sixty minutes after the start time is not considered being late. We also came to realize that dinner usually doesn't start before seven and can easily go until all hours of the night (like midnight on a school night!). Therefore, we found that meeting at an outside venue would usually offer us greater flexibility, especially if we needed to leave early.

When hosting a book club or Bible study, I've intentionally elected to meet up at a coffee shop or a restaurant. While I love opening my home, I also appreciate making things easier for myself. If I pick a location where I as the hostess just have to show up and don't have as much to do before and after, it saves me both time and energy. By picking outside venues I'm able to host more often because it costs me less all around. I'm purposefully decreasing my workload and therefore increasing my available time for building community. One other benefit is that life at home can continue to flow—people still get to soccer practice and homework is able to get done. My event doesn't distract from what is a "normal" day for the rest of my household.

If you work long hours and don't have the time or energy to prepare your home for guests, then don't force it. If you have a houseful of roommates and don't feel like you have the space or privacy to host, then choose to host and meet up elsewhere. If you find it challenging to host because you have young kids, then why not opt for a kid-friendly venue where the kids can run free? If you find managing your pets when you have guests over to be too much work, then leave your pets at home and ask your guests to meet you at a different location. If it's hard for you to relax when you host in your home, gather somewhere else and see if that helps.

Gathering somewhere other than your home doesn't have to mean less connectivity. A home can feel warm and inviting, but so can many other venues. Meeting at the park, the library, a restaurant, or even doing an activity together are all ways to coordinate a get-together without having to do so in your home. If you find that you don't host much in your home (for whatever reason), think about which outside venues might be good fits for you. As the host you can pick the venue, so pick the one that works for you!

Your Hurdle: Where

When you gather, whether inside or outside your home, remember to focus on the true currency: the relationships. Also be sure to honor your life season and the range of hospitality personalities within your home; consider everyone you live with when deciding whether to host in your home.

When you do open your door, continue to recognize that your hosting is an extension of the condition of your heart. If you are at peace with your choice, this will translate to your guests and their experience.

Connecting is what lasts and makes memories. Connection is what truly matters, no matter the location. It's all about the shared experience; nobody really cares if you use plastic utensils and paper plates. But if you have the chance and can do so, consider adding some tiki lights!

Think about a time when you've been to someone's home and felt completely at ease. What made you feel that way? What elements were a part of that experience (specifically in the host's home or with the host's attitude/demeanor)? What helped you to unwind and relax?

107

_____

_____

_____

_____

_____

_____

_____

Share about a time when you've been to a gathering at an outside venue and you've had a wonderful time. What about the venue helped make you feel that way? What factors were a part of that experience that made it possible for you to settle in and enjoy yourself?

_____

_____

_____

_____

_____

_____

CHAPTER ELEVEN

when

time

When we relocated from New Mexico back to Oregon, I was busy unpacking, drowning amid boxes and packing paper, and I heard the doorbell ring. I went to the door and there on the step was a surprise gift. It was a beautiful plant with a card attached. The gift was from our new next-door neighbor, Christy. Inside the card she had written kind words welcoming us to the neighborhood and included the names of everyone in her family and their children's ages. This gracious gesture opened the door for a budding friendship. Christy was an exceptional neighbor and was always gathering people together. I learned a lot from her about how to host and how to be a gift to your neighbors. I feel blessed that I was able to be her neighbor, even though it wasn't nearly long enough! (When they told us they were moving, and only a mile or two away, David about had a meltdown. Good neighbors are a blessing!)

It would have been easier for Christy to just sit back and wait until we had maybe bumped into each other or passed one another while out on a walk. But instead of sitting back, she took the initiative. She made hospitality a priority and created the time to extend a heartfelt welcome. This is a great aim! Hospitality should be a goal and when you plan it within your schedule, it will help you to better match your calendar to your hosting commitments.

As you leap over the next hosting hurdle, the "when," it's important to honor your hospitality personality and also the different demands on your schedule. Hospitality may be gifted 24/7, which is the cool part. However, the complicated part can be knowing when to schedule or when to be spontaneous. There are times for each, and your responsibility is to know when to do which.

Don't worry, it's not a formula. It's choosing to have a heart of hospitality and making the choice to be other centered. Really, that's it!

Small-Picture View

The small-picture view is the time within your twenty-four hours each day. In every day there are small moments available for you to extend hospitality. No matter how jam-packed your calendar might be, you still have a minute here and a minute there. Within these small minutes and moments, there are ways to offer hospitality.

In your home, this may involve saying a kind compliment to someone unexpectedly, taking out the trash without being asked, or putting something away where it belongs. In your work, this may be supporting a coworker with your time or attention, demonstrating humility (even when it's challenging to do so), or asking how you may be of help to someone. Throughout your day, this may be recognizing opportunities to help others around you, those who are directly in front of you, whether planned or unplanned. You might ask if someone needs help carrying something, or acknowledge someone rather than keeping your head down and staying inside your head or—dare I say?—staring at your screen.

When you think of the small-picture view, the "when" is each moment in front of you. By making a deliberate choice to be less inwardly focused and more outwardly focused, you may be surprised by the abundance of opportunities that are available all around you! When you remain more focused on others it will help you experience increased connection within your communities. Entertainers, you are naturally very friendly and outgoing—use this gift. Includers, you are warm and caring; you know how to make others feel noticed—keep this up! Leaders, you are likely to initiate and open the door to relationships—your boldness is a blessing. Organizers, you are very detail-oriented; use this strength to help discover the ways you can best connect with others.

In many ways, the small-picture view of hospitality is really what I would consider to be the easiest form of hospitality, as it doesn't usually require much preparation. You simply do what you are able to do in the moment. Like the kind gentlemen who stepped up and helped my daughter with her car when it wouldn't start or the generous person who bought my drink ahead of me at the drive-thru or my friendly neighbor who always greeted me with gusto when she drove by. None of these experiences were prepared ahead of time. Instead they reflect people being intentional and taking advantage of the moment in front of them.

Hospitality is the friendly reception and treatment of guests or strangers. Therefore, demonstrating hospitality should be our attitude and approach 24/7. We should be actively looking for ways to be warm, friendly, and generous. We should be moving through our days seeking ways to love and serve others.

If you pay more attention to the small events that are already available throughout your day, you will be able to make your hospitality even more of a daily occurrence. I pray this will be a radical change for you. That you will have a fresh view and see hospitality in a new way. That you will seek out instances where you can give and share within your smallest moments, within your day-to-day. That you will treat hospitality as a gift that you can offer at every turn!

Big-Picture View

Christy's kind gift took planning. She had to buy the plant and card, fill out the card, and then deliver it to us. This wasn't a spontaneous form of hospitality. It required some forethought. And many forms of hospitality do fall under this umbrella. Hoping that things will happen, or that you will have an excuse to host, isn't a strategy. Preparing is important and has a place when gifting hospitality. From a big-picture view, or what I'll refer to as more of a weekly or monthly view, you'll want to evaluate when hosting and attending things fits best within your schedule.

If you work Monday through Friday, then hosting a dinner party on a Friday evening in your home may not be the best option. Maybe you could host at a different venue or look at a Saturday night instead? If you prefer to go to bed earlier rather than later, factor this in when planning to host. You'll want to make sure that you have enough energy to enjoy your time and be fully engaged. If you love breaking up your week by having something to look forward to, then accepting the invite to the weeknight monthly Bunco group or book club may be a fantastic fit for you. When something isn't every single week and falls instead on a monthly or rotating basis, it can often feel more manageable.

Setting up your hosting and attending schedule, weekly and monthly, will require that you look at your calendar in its entirety. Taking into consideration the other demands on your time and the times of the day that are the most natural for you to socialize will help you better determine when you want (and don't want) to host, as well as when to say yes (or no) to an invite. Also be sensitive to whether you are having more of an open or closed home right now, your professional or personal demands, and where you fall on the introvert and extrovert continuum.

Your Hurdle: When

Leaders and Entertainers can tend to have a high capacity for socializing. If this is you, you will want to work on being considerate of your counterparts. Your plus-one or friend may not want to socialize as long as you do. Includers and Organizers can tend to need more downtime or may have stronger preferences as to when they want to socialize. If this is you, you will want to make sure you are using healthy boundaries.

As with all aspects of hospitality, remember that there are always at least two parties involved. Acknowledging the time that will work best for both the guest and the host is a great starting point. It can't always be achieved, but it is a thoughtful way to show consideration and can also maximize the ability to connect when you do get together.

Additionally, I want to encourage you to be a flexible host. The "when" shouldn't be the most important factor. If you can't gather on Christmas Day as a family, you can still celebrate together—even if it needs to be scheduled a week later. If you have to plan a group birthday party in order to recognize several family members at one time, then do so! If you are called to help someone and it's not necessarily convenient but you are available, then you should help.

Put on your hospitality glasses and look for opportunities to be kind and generous at every turn. Deliberately schedule hospitality on your calendar, and make a commitment to honor your own personal limitations. When you respect your time, your schedule, and your hospitality personality, you will be able to honor yourself and others. You will be able to give them your full attention and care. You will be able to serve them well.

> Put on your hospitality glasses and look for opportunities to be kind and generous at every turn.

In the small-picture view, when have you gifted spontaneous hospitality or received it? How did it make you feel?

_____

_____

_____

_____

_____

_____

In the big-picture view, when do you prefer to host or socialize (have the energy to entertain, spend time with others, or give of yourself)?

_____

_____

_____

_____

_____

_____

CHAPTER TWELVE

why

love

You and I are called to love others. This is the "why" behind our extension of hospitality. We were created to be in community. As human beings we were formed to want to be with others and to not live our lives in isolation. We desire intimacy and we want to be known.

Love is a choice, and it doesn't always come as naturally as we may want it to. We can have roadblocks (which might sometimes look like self-focus) that keep us stuck. We can have good intentions that often just remain thoughts or ideas. We can have suffocating insecurities, lingering doubts, and fears of rejection. But I believe Jesus knows all about rejection, and if he calls me to love, then I'm going to step forward in faith. If I can love others more by being hospitable, then I'm going to do my best. I want to shine his love and hope to this world. I don't want to contribute to more isolation. I'd rather be a champion for togetherness. I'm of the opinion that we're better together! Jesus emphasized this when he was asked which were the greatest commandments: "'Love the Lord your God with all your heart and with all your soul and with all your mind and with all your strength.' The second is this: 'Love your neighbor as yourself'" (Mark 12:30–31).

In her TED talk, author and speaker Shasta Nelson states that in order to have healthy intimate relationships (or what she calls *frientimacy*) there needs to be three components: positivity, consistency, and vulnerability. She states, "Because at the end of the day, for us, we want to feel loved, and we only feel loved if we feel known, and we can only feel known if we actually share ourselves."[1]

We have to show up for each other, and most importantly, open our hearts.

A common symbol of hospitality is the pineapple. This originated in history when pineapples were rare and harder to find, which therefore meant that they were also in higher demand. There are different stories as to how the pineapple specifically relates to hospitality, but according to *Southern Living*, here are two explanations:

The Tradition: The ability of a hostess to have a pineapple adorn her dining table for an important event said as much about her rank in society as it did about her ingenuity. These beautiful fruits were in such high demand, but so hard to get, that colonial confectioners would often rent them to households by the day. Later, the same fruit was sold to other, more affluent clients who actually ate it. While fruits in general—fresh, dried, candied and jellied—were in great demand, the pineapple was the true celebrity. Its rarity, expense, and striking beauty made it the ultimate exotic fruit. Visitors confronted with pineapple-topped food displays felt particularly honored by a hostess who obviously spared no expense to ensure her guests' dining pleasure. In this manner, the image of the pineapple came to express the sense of hospitality characteristic of gracious home gatherings.

The Legend: The sea captains of New England traded among the Caribbean Islands, returning to the colonies bearing their heavy cargoes of spices, rum, and a selection of fruits, which sometimes included pineapples. According to the legend, the captain would drop anchor in the harbor and see to his cargo and crew. Once his work was done, he would head home, stopping outside his house to spear a pineapple on a fence post. This would let his friends know of his safe return from sea. The pineapple was an invitation for them to visit, share his food and drink, and listen to tales of his voyage.[2]

What rings true in both of these stories is that the pineapple was a visible reminder of a desire to gather together. *The pineapple was saying welcome!*

The hostess used her ability to find a pineapple, and in doing so demonstrated how much she honored and valued her guests. She was sharing that she had gone above and beyond to prepare for them. She wanted to give her very best. The pineapple proudly on display represented her effort and thoughtfulness. The sea captain used the pineapple as a way to express an invitation. It revealed not only that he had returned home safe from his journey but also that he wished to see his friends again. His home was open. He desired to reconnect and share stories. Both the hostess and the captain wanted to share their gifts with their guests. They wanted to extend hospitality. They were placing an importance on their relationships by using a symbol that represented a sacrifice.

Love (hospitality), at the core, is you and me choosing to focus outwardly rather than inwardly.

In *Loving My Actual Neighbor*, Alex Kuykendall describes how to practically and purposefully love your neighbors.

We have this God-gifted thing we call "free will," the ability to make choices within the constraints of our actual lives. We can choose to take a posture of humility, to ask questions and sincerely listen, to be in the uncomfortable and not try to change what we cannot, to bring warmth and generosity to our neighbors. No matter the location—apartment to cul-de-sac, city block to country road—God has given us choices in these matters. It is our time to make them. He has also remarkably given us the choice to live out these practices with our neighbors regardless of who we are and who they are. It may be easier for some of us than others to practice the practices, but we always have the choice.[3]

My challenge to you is this: Seek to love others—your family, friends, coworkers, neighbors, acquaintances, strangers. Look for ways to share hospitality within every one of your circles. Find opportunities to offer both secret and spontaneous hospitality! By doing so, you will be supplying to others what they need the most.

There is a high demand and desire for connectivity. However, the sad reality is that loneliness has become an epidemic in America, and for various reasons. "One in four Americans rarely or never feel as though there are people who understand them. Two in five Americans sometimes or always feel that their relationships are not meaningful and that they are isolated from others. And one in five people report they rarely or never feel close to people or feel like there are people they can talk to."[4]

People are lonely. Let's not stay complacent, pulling into our garages and shutting the door immediately or keeping our heads down so that we don't have to make eye contact or engage. I want you and I to love our neighbors. I want us to spread hope and welcome others with our love. We can choose to open our doors, share kindness, give generously, *and express our love.* By sharing our time and attention we can foster friendship, build connection, and create community. We can use our hospitality to share our love and Jesus's love. We can make a choice to be *positive, consistent, and vulnerable.*

I love going home to visit my parents. Both are wonderful hosts. I thankfully had a really good example of how to love well and gather people together.

My dad is known for stashing candy and goodies into the cup holders of the car when he picks us up from the airport. Even I get excited and feel loved by his efforts. My mom goes out of her way to set up our guest rooms, remembering everything from boxes of tissues to extra toothpaste, even a cup and pitcher of water on the nightstand. And she also plans the best menus that I always look forward to devouring. (Why is it that when someone else cooks for you it always tastes better than when you make it?) While I know my parents love me deeply, these added touches continue to show me their love in a tangible way. Their prepared-ness and thoughtfulness reveal that they were thinking about us, anticipating our visit, and want to make us feel welcomed. They are welcoming us in love.

Your Hurdle: Why

When you think about how your hospitality personality allows you to love others, keep in mind that others want your gifts of hospitality. Others need you to focus on them. Others need you to notice them. Others need your kindness, compassion, and love. You have much to give, and when you give you will bless and be blessed. You have time, talents, and treasures to share, and many who want to receive these very things from you.

Let's always remember the *why* behind our hospitality—it's love, plain and simple.

However, genuine and sincere hospitality can often be in high demand and low supply, much like the pineapple used to be. Let's work to minimize this gap. You and me. Let's commit to creating a hospitality chain reaction. Let's maximize connection and community, starting today!

> Others need you to focus on them. Others need your kindness, compassion, and love.

As a Jesus follower, I want to keep jumping over my hospitality hurdles (no matter how high they might feel) so I can faithfully love others. Loving God and loving people: that is my aim.

What are some of the struggles you have when it comes to extending an invitation or reaching out to someone?

_____

_____

_____

When have you felt loved by someone's gift of hospitality?

_____

_____

_____

List some practical and tangible ways you could share more love with others.

_____

_____

_____

your
hospitality
hang-ups

*But entertaining isn't a sport or a competition. It's an act of love,
if you let it be. You can twist it and turn it into anything you
want—a way to show off your house, a way to compete with your
friends, a way to earn love and approval. Or you can decide that
every time you open your door, it's an act of love, not performance
or competition or striving. You can decide that every time people
gather around your table, your goal is nourishment, not neurotic
proving. You can decide.*

Shauna Niequist

CHAPTER THIRTEEN

connection

fellowship and fumbles

When it comes to hosting and initiating connection, we can and will most likely experience some hang-ups. These hospitality hang-ups can manifest before, during, or after hosting (or in all three situations). Hang-ups affect your enjoyment when extending hospitality to others. They can look and feel like stress, hurt feelings, anxiety, boredom, exhaustion, and vulnerability. While you and I can't necessarily avoid every hosting hang-up, we can better prepare and anticipate the realities of some of the common ones. In this section, I'm going to dive into topics ranging from fellowship, to food planning, to the functionality of your home/space. I want to help equip you to more fully enjoy sharing your hospitality gifts with others. The following chapters will hopefully give you more confidence with your hosting and give you permission to connect, collaborate, and get cozy.

For our daughter's last season of high school swim team, we agreed to host an early-morning breakfast for the entire team. Prior to the event, I pictured the girls (all forty-five of them) lounging around in our great room, snacking and enjoying delicious breakfast foods, with me capturing the moments by snapping pictures. David and I would be smiling, serving them, and most certainly soaking up the memory.

Well, here's how things really looked. While making the three nine-by-thirteen casserole-style quiches, I discarded the twenty-seven eggshells (like I normally do) right into the garbage disposal. (I'm a clean-as-you-go kind of cook.) We realized minutes before the swim team arrived that our garbage disposal had stopped working and the sink was clogged and full of eggshells and water. David was shocked (and maybe just a little bit irritated) to learn that I had put that many eggshells down the garbage disposal. Honestly, I didn't know that you couldn't or shouldn't do this.

While he worked with the shop vacuum to suction the standing water out of the sink, I worked to blend the breakfast smoothies. However, when I went to transfer the drink (an Orange Julius concoction) from the blender to a large decanter (one of those with a pretty stand and spout), I discovered that the liquid was too thick to actually move through the spout. I then had to scramble and transfer the smoothie mixture into some pitchers instead, which also meant more mess. We rushed to clean up the disasters, tucked the vacuum out of sight, and wiped down the counters. Then we switched gears, opened the front door, and welcomed the girls into our home. The team had come straight from practice and they were starving!

The quiches were gone in a flash, and as I surveyed the scene I realized that there were only four pancakes remaining and still about fifteen girls in line. I frantically looked for David and told him to get back to the kitchen! We needed more pancakes—stat! (He's the breakfast guy at our house.) While he rushed to get more pancakes made, I kept thinking to myself how glad I was that at the last minute I had decided to buy a dozen muffins from Costco. Having backup food is always a good idea!

After the second batch of pancakes was served and the garbage can was overflowing, the house was suddenly empty again. After a whirlwind of activity that barely lasted thirty minutes, it was over. Well, except for the cleanup. David and I looked at each other, laughed, and then started to tidy things up. Memories were definitely made and lessons both learned and reinforced.

It's easy to anticipate things with an idealistic mindset. We can paint a picture in our mind (without even meaning to) of how we hope the time we plan to spend with others might look. We can find ourselves longing for laughter, seeking positivity, and ultimately, hoping that everyone will connect and click well. And while sometimes this is the case, it's not always the reality. We need to include space for understanding, gentleness, and respect.

The outcome of hosting the girls' swim team was not necessarily what we had anticipated. All in all, we did what we said we would do, and hopefully we showed our love to the girls by providing a hot breakfast and modeling that we as a couple, and as parents, clearly do not have everything together. *Welcome to our home! We're doing our best and we try to do it with a joyful spirit despite any (and all) setbacks!*

When it comes to fellowship, start by identifying your individual mission for each time you host. When you know the intention for your hospitality, or your event, and the form of fellowship you are hoping to create, you will be able to more fully realize the joy of the experience. A prepared mindset will help you to remember your why.

Fellowship

Fellowship is usually experienced in one of three ways. *Outward hospitality* often transpires when you are mentoring, leading, or giving. *Mutual hospitality* occurs when you are socializing with those you share common interests and values with (most likely those in your inner circle). And *inward hospitality* takes place when you are being cared for or nurtured by someone else. In order to thrive in each of these areas, it's important to identify when you are in each experience and the specific role you play.

Outward Hospitality

When hosting the swim team breakfast, David and I knew we were there simply to facilitate the overall experience. We were offering our hospitality and our home for the swim team's benefit. As an Organizer, I was all about the details—although I did mistakenly underestimate how hungry the girls would be! And David, as an Entertainer, took the lack of pancakes in stride and was quick to make jokes and laugh at himself over the obvious hosting hiccup. We didn't have any big expectations of connecting with the girls or feel the need to add much in the way of entertainment or engagement. Those pieces were already built in, because the girls were an established and close-knit group. All they really needed from us was a place to load up paper plates with hot breakfast foods and some chairs and couches to crash on to create a "team" memory.

In an effort to be sensitive and respectful, we put our pets away, told our two younger kids they needed to stay in their rooms, and stepped out of the kitchen when we could in an effort to give the girls their space. This was a time to serve and, if possible, remain unseen because the event was about them. We were practicing outward hospitality.

There are times with outward hospitality that you may be required to be more hands-on, like when hosting a baby shower or a fundraising event. There are other times when you may be more hands-off. Like the night I agreed to let Ainsley host a backyard summer party at our house and then found myself cooped up in our bedroom for hours wondering when the party would finally end. It wasn't convenient for me or comfortable, but it was important for me to encourage my daughter to live her mission of loving others and welcoming her friends into our home. I was able to give outward hospitality by sacrificing my own wants and needs and agreeing to be the designated chaperone (hiding and tucked away upstairs). I chose to enjoy the hang-up, because I was focused on the bigger vision of supporting my daughter. There will be times when you are on the front lines with outward hospitality and times when you are working behind the scenes. Both are equally important and necessary.

Outward hospitality may feel inconvenient and like it comes more at a cost. This form of hospitality can often be more a time of giving than receiving. Make sure to honor yourself and know when to say yes and when to say no—recognizing that if your cup runs dry, you won't have much to give. Avoid the tendency to focus all your hospitality outwardly. It's equally important for you to focus on the other two forms, mutual and inward hospitality. Knowing when you are required to extend outward hospitality will help you avoid common hosting hang-ups. You'll be clear and confident in your role and able to better enjoy your time hosting because of a defined vision for your time.

Mutual Hospitality

One year we hosted Thanksgiving and invited some other families to join us. We told them to either bring prepared dishes, or they could plan to cook things once they arrived. One of our friends, Nick, showed up with five grocery bags full of all kinds of foods. As he unpacked his goods, I saw that he had taken our "bring your own foods" instruction very seriously. He seemed to unpack every spice bottle he owned and then began to dice and slice an enormous pile of vegetables. It was during this time that I stepped out of the kitchen and found the floppy turkey hat (that he had also brought) and put it on, realizing that I wasn't going to be needed much in the kitchen. A win for me! I love mutual hospitality.

Mutual hospitality is *all hands on deck*! This form of fellowship may look like two couples getting together for dinner, or girlfriends meeting up for a Girls' Night Out at their favorite restaurant, or a group of guys gathering to watch a game, or parents showing up at the park to watch their kids play on the playground. It often occurs when there is already some familiarity, usually with those you consider to be in your inner circle—people you are already connected with.

With mutual hospitality you might feel the freedom to take a more relaxed approach—especially if you are hosting family members you are in close relationship with or friends you consider to be your besties. It's often in these forms of hosting that you'll feel more than OK if your kids are running around like wild animals, if your dog won't get off the couch, or if your floors are majorly overdue for a cleaning. When you fellowship in a mutual way, you'll still honor your guests, but you will also be able to relax and embrace the freedom that comes with letting your guests step in and help.

Here are some ideas for delegating to create fellowship that focuses on mutual hospitality:

- See if your friend the Includer would be willing to create the guest list and also extend the invites. (She'll be thrilled you asked!)
- Ask one guest to be in charge of the entertainment. Maybe they could bring a board game, a movie, or an activity to do together. This would most certainly be a great job to assign to an Entertainer!
- Request that everyone bring a dish to share. This will lighten your meal prep work and allow for others to share their cooking/baking gifts. You could even ask your friend, maybe a Leader, to help coordinate this piece.
- When guests arrive, ask one person to make the salad and another person to set the table. While it's nice to have everything ready (hello, Organizers!), it's also fun to work together and set a tone of teamwork and camaraderie

128

(Includers love this!). By involving everyone or giving them a "job," it can actually help people feel more at ease.

- Allow your guests to help you with the cleanup. (Don't require it, but don't turn away their help either.) Again, this gives them a job.

Delegating not only helps lighten your load, it also pulls everyone together. When a guest has something to do, it helps them feel more settled and like they have a place. And in turn this will often help you as the host to feel more settled because the details are all being attended to. Make sure you are sensitive about who you delegate things to. You want to play to your guests' strengths. Set each of them up for success and give them a job that best matches their abilities. (For example, you wouldn't want me to broil the bread; it's not my forte!)

Mutual hospitality can be life-giving and meaningful to both parties. It's a beautiful blend of you and me. This is what our Thanksgiving celebration was with our good friends. We all pitched in to do the dishes after we ate, took turns watching each other's kids, and then lined up side by side to pack up the leftovers. We were mutually seeking fellowship. There was a give-and-take, and plenty of spices to go around. This was a perfect example of a "Friendsgiving," and there's no reason to limit this to only once a year!

> Mutual hospitality can be life-giving and meaningful to both parties. It's a beautiful blend of you and me.

Inward Hospitality

When you find yourself in a time of crisis or a major life change has rocked your world, you may have less energy or ability to look outside of yourself. If your current season or situation makes hosting or hospitality not viable options, or you need to (for a time) be more inward focused, this is OK. Give yourself permission to take a hosting break. The fact that you can recognize your present reality is so healthy and important. Knowing your capacities and capabilities is rule number one if you desire to be a healthy host.

Inward hospitality is the reminder on the flight of life to put your own oxygen mask on first.

This may mean allowing others to bring you meals or asking friends to help watch your kids or saying yes when someone offers to do something that you could or would normally do for yourself. It may mean taking some personal time off work, building in more time for your self-care, or accepting help even when you don't want to. It was me accepting my dear friend Jamie's offer to brush my hair. I allowed her to love on me and care for me. It was our family being open to receiving help and accepting meals for an entire month after having our third baby. Our community rallied and we accepted. I still remember many of the meals that were brought to us, and I have warm feelings from receiving so much support. Our friends provided nourishment for us at a time when we really needed it.

Inward hospitality is being true to yourself and your needs, and then allowing others to bless you with their gifts of hospitality. Welcome their offerings, and yes, also use the necessary boundaries. (There are some great tips in chapter 16 about how to receive help during a time of need.) Just because you need help or need to receive from others doesn't mean that you have to say yes to every offer that is presented. Whatever you are struggling with or need help with, remain as humble as possible and allow others to extend their outward hospitality to you. There is a time to give and a time to receive.

Fumbles

When you open your door, extend an invitation, or coordinate a gathering, there is always the possibility of problems. Fumbles can often add to the experience or memory—sometimes positively and other times negatively. While we don't necessarily want to invite party fouls, they do seem to find their way in!

I wish that when my queso attempt hadn't turned out at my daughter's third birthday party that I would have been less concerned about my lack of knowledge. I wish I could have been able to laugh at myself. But instead I chose to overreact and become defensive, frankly because I was embarrassed. What if instead I had found the humor in it? What if I had dropped off gifts of (store-bought) queso to my friends the next day as a way to help keep things light and fun? What if I had been easier on myself and not taken myself so seriously? What if . . . ?

When things go wrong, whether it's queso that doesn't look like queso, a pet that won't behave, standing water in the sink, a toilet that won't flush, a new scratch on your table, spilled milk, or unruly kids, you can always choose to pivot toward positivity. You can intentionally move in the direction of not taking things so seriously.

Things go wrong, period. It happens to all of us. No one is immune to mistakes, misses, and messes. I love my friend Kristen's example of working through a hosting hang-up during her daughter's sorority friends' visit to their home.

Coats and boots scattered across the entryway, pillows and blankets covering much of upstairs, cups and cell phones all over the kitchen counters, and too many suitcases, bags and purses to count filled every surface in my daughter's room (and the hallway outside my husband's office). This kind of clutter can crawl up and down my skin. Add in loud, late nights, and this early-to-bed girl can begin to fall apart. Throw in a snow storm that begs me to make 16 lunches out of four baking potatoes for the unexpected extra meal at home and I should be totally undone!

While I've always liked having people over and considered hospitality a gift, as grace has worked its way through me I realize how I think about hospitality has changed too. No longer is it about entertaining, but about inviting. Serving, giving, one anothering. It's not about me . . . what my house looks like, how much money I have, how good a cook I may be, what Pinterest displays I've successfully mastered.

When we open our homes, we have the opportunity to welcome others into our hearts and usher in grace to theirs. But this can be missed if we put up the facade of perfection through our production. When we are more focused on the event, the details, the trying to make things perfect, we can unintentionally create a barrier between us and our guests, instead of an invitation to share ourselves in a way that leads to true fellowship and rejuvenation.[1]

Due to an unexpected snowstorm, Kristen's guests were housebound and hungry. Not only was Kristen able to pivot, by making a large batch of baked potato soup—with only four potatoes on hand—she kept her focus on fostering fellowship.

Let's be like Kristen. Rally when we need to rally. Say yes, even when it's a stretch. Remember that people want to be invited. Be willing to roll with what comes our way. Recognize that there will always be some form of bless in the mess!

And take note, whatever your hospitality personality, it's always good to have a backup plan. Whether that means keeping pizzas in your freezer or knowing the number for a good takeout option, be ready to change direction and respond. (Or in Kristen's case, know how to make soup for sixteen with only four potatoes!)

Organizers and Leaders can tend to struggle more when things go awry as they generally are natural planners (I think Kristen and I can both relate to this). We can feel and think that if we plan well enough then things will naturally go well. If you find yourself in this predicament, make a point to look to your Entertainers and Includers. They are usually excellent at shifting with any and all setbacks. Going with the flow is their motto. They actually tend to thrive when things go wrong, or not as planned. They are good at keeping their stress levels in check and knowing how to roll through hosting hiccups. Whatever your hospitality personality, work to manage the tensions as they build to avoid added stress while you are hosting.

> Have you ever been to a party where the host is stressed and uptight? Or is so behind schedule that she is frantically running around trying to finish the preparations as the guests are arriving? It is an uncomfortable feeling for the guests and sets the wrong tone for the party. Does this mean everything has to be perfect and there are never any stressful moments in entertaining? No, of course not. *Remember, do a few things and do them well.* If something goes wrong (the icemaker breaks, the smoke alarm goes off, one of the dishes you will serve has taken a turn for the worse), don't panic. Simply solve the problem and move on. The ability to be flexible and not let it ruin your evening is a plus. Put a smile on your face and enjoy your guests and your party.[2]

When you remain comfortable with whatever comes your way, then your guests will mirror your behavior. In my experience, I have found that a flexible host is usually a more fun host!

If your food doesn't turn out, or the ambiance isn't what you were hoping for, or the conversation feels stagnant, you as the host can still work to set a tone of comfort. With fellowship and fumbles, remember the goal of hospitality is always love. It is showing you care and working to build relationships. Use your hospitality personality to honor the event and the people you are celebrating.

Entertainers, make sure to focus on being other centered. Leaders, respect the desires of those who the event is intended for. Includers, work to understand what your boundaries need to be. And Organizers, strive to let go of control—when required. By honoring the intention for your hosting and any hang-ups or hiccups that may come your way, you will be able to experience more joy and ultimately, more connection.

Share about a time when you showed outward hospitality.

_____

_____

_____

Share about a time when you were a part of mutual hospitality.

_____

_____

_____

Share about a time when you were extended inward hospitality.

_____

_____

_____

Share about a time when you had to roll through a hosting fumble.

_____

_____

_____

CHAPTER FOURTEEN

collaboration

food and finances

For several years, while living in Oregon, I was involved in our neighborhood Bunco group. As a young mom, I loved those nights "out" and "off." I would very much look forward to walking over to my neighbor's house, catching up with the other ladies, and munching on the yummy foods. However, when it was MY night to host, which was typically only once a year, I usually didn't share the same feelings. Instead, I would stress out over the menu, spend lots of time cleaning up my house, and the day of the event I could be found running around looking like a chicken with her head cut off. Maybe this was because my kids were younger? Maybe this was because we hosted a full meal that included appetizers, a main dish, and a dessert? Maybe this was because I was a relatively unexperienced hostess? Or maybe a combination of all three?

Nonetheless, just last week I hosted a neighborhood Bunco group here in my current home, in Colorado, and I felt the same way. (And my kids for the most part are now self-sufficient.) I rushed around the day prior and the day of, shopping for easy-to-make appetizers, buying candies for the tables, and choosing which drinks to serve. Then I spent the afternoon wiping down kitchen counters and appliances, cleaning the powder bath, and vacuuming like it was my j-o-b, all between driving for soccer carpool, sweeping the front porch, and trying to find some last-minute substitute players because we were short.

You know what's hard about hosting? The work that happens behind the scenes. There is the food (the planning) and the finances (the spending), and both are usually parts of the hosting equation, no matter what the occasion may look like. They come into play either at your home or an outside venue.

So let's talk about how to keep the planning and the spending in their proper place and within a healthy hosting perspective. We need to maintain a realistic approach, with both food and finances, to avoid hosting hang-ups along the way.

Food

As you've processed whether you are more of a foodie or a non-foodie, continue to give yourself permission to make things work for you when it comes to the menu and food planning. If you are a raving fan of cooking and creating menus, then carry on! If you are not a fan of all things kitchen related, then outsource! If you are somewhere in the middle, find a balance between serving some things homemade and some things store-bought. All combinations can and will work. You decide. Then, let's all remember to give grace. Both to those who love the kitchen and the menu planning and to those who prefer to opt for store-bought or takeout.

Even though I had attempted to make things easy for myself, when hosting my current Bunco group, I did end up overbuying, overpreparing, and overserving. The food was barely touched at the end of the evening. However, what did bring me joy was that as a group we had a conversation about the need to simplify the menu for our times together. Our Bunco group had recently formed, and

I was thankful that we were able to have an open conversation about some of the details and yes, the *expectations*. We decided as a group to streamline things and clarified that future hosts would need to offer only a small amount of food. One or two options would be sufficient; most of us weren't coming hungry because most of us had just finished eating dinner. It was important to better define the expectations. Our conversation will be helpful for all of the group's future hosts. Based on some new and clarified guidelines, each host will also be able to save both time and money, and hopefully experience less stress!

Sometimes we don't talk enough about expectations, and I think this can be a miss. We continue to do things the way they have always been done rather than stepping back, reevaluating, discussing, and even taking a vote. Continued conversations about what's working and not working are so helpful, especially when we seek to grow closer in community and connection. Don't be afraid to gently spur these conversations on. It's OK to talk about things! (Often others want to and will be thankful when a topic is finally brought to light.) Work to gently specify expectations and intentions rather than staying stuck in assumption. *Why go above and beyond if that's not what people want or need?*

I will still probably stress somewhat when preparing to host a Bunco night. First, because it usually falls in the middle of a school/work week. And second, because I will most likely still feel the need to do some tidying

> Sometimes we don't talk enough about expectations.

up. I am thankful, however, that the food portion of this event has become even more manageable thanks to our open dialogue.

Food has a place, but what needs to be prioritized more are the people you invite. They need to feel included, accepted, and cared for. Your hospitality emphasis should be centered on creating the space and time for connection. I don't know about you, but I always appreciate when someone asks me to spend time with them. I don't care if they offer to make me a sandwich at their kitchen counter, want to serve me a special homemade dinner, or simply ask to meet up for a cup of coffee. *The food is secondary; the connection is primary.*

That said, there are little things you can do that make a big impact. You'll enjoy reading the hosting themes (chap. 17) and getting some great tips (chap. 16) for how to add a little punch to your parties in some simple and impactful ways. Food can be simple and very satisfying! As is adding small touches like white butcher paper, fresh flowers, or a fun playlist.

By creating a theme or setting a tone you will be showing your guests that you have been preparing for them and anticipating your time together. Addition, such as placing name tags on the table, lighting candles, or playing music that ties into your theme, are all welcoming ways to contribute to a meaningful experience.

But please, let yourself off the hook when it comes to the food. Don't make it a big deal. Instead, make a really big deal about the people who you get to do life with! They will appreciate this so much more. Remember, takeout is always a great option! Who says you can't order pizza? And who is "who," anyway?

Finances

All right, let's talk money. Financial costs are a factor of hosting and yes, they too can be a hang-up. If you are in a life season where you don't have extra or have lots of demands within your budget, then the idea of buying food, decorations, or anything you need to host may feel overwhelming or out of reach. I get it. I struggle with this at times too. Serving others can be costly, and it may often feel like the opportunity to host doesn't come at a good time—specifically when matched with your financial obligations, goals, and responsibilities.

As a host, be realistic about what your hosting budget needs to look like and then work within those parameters. To stretch your budget when hosting, practice simplicity and don't overdo things. *Generous hospitality is more about being present than about the presentation anyway.* Like with your food planning, be wise and intentional with your budgeting. Find ways to be creative. Simplify where you can and take the pressure off yourself. The food, decorations, and entertainment are all extras and not always necessary.

- Do I recommend you set a budget for hosting? Yes.
- Do I suggest you consider the costs of planning a gathering? Yes.
- Do I support you spreading the workload to help with the financial load? Yes.

I overpurchased for my Bunco gathering, but you know what? It was somewhat intentional, even though it may not have looked that way. All the food items I bought could and would be eaten by my household should there be leftovers. Which is exactly what happened.

When the ladies left that night, I sent a group text to my "Tribe Tyree" that said, "If you want food come and get it!" Within minutes my kitchen island was lined with my three kids and my husband. They all started making plates and were thrilled to have access to the delicious appetizers. And the best news of all is that it meant I got a couple of nights off from cooking! I just kept bringing out the appetizers night after night until they were gone.

To help minimize some of the hang-ups (stress, time, and money) that are often associated with hosting, here are some ways to creatively host. Each of these ideas can help spread the workload and decrease the direct demand (for food and finances) on the host.

- *Potluck Style*: There's a reason these are so popular! Each person brings what they like to eat, and there is naturally something for everyone. It also creates variety and makes the planning and preparing easier for the host.

- *"BYO" Barbeque Style*: This is a great way to gather in the summer. Everyone can enjoy their preferred choice of barbeque. The host provides the barbeque equipment and may prepare side dishes or divvy those up as well.

- *Picnic Style*: Join up at the park, go to a summer concert, or meet for a hike. This way it's a brown bag lunch or a picnic dinner. Each person brings their own packed meal. The host may coordinate when and where, but the "what to bring" is then left up to the individual.

- *Cook-off Style*: Make it a competition! Choose a theme, like "best pizza" or "best grilled cheese sandwich," then invite everyone to bring their own ingredients and specialties. Do a cook-off taste test, and then have everyone vote for their favorite.

- *Activity Style*: Choose to go bowling or bike riding or play tennis. By meeting up at an outside venue (somewhere like a bowling alley or health club) you'll often have the option of food provided at the facility and this will take the food planning out of the equation.

- *One Course Style*: Only serve appetizers and drinks or host a dessert and game night. Remove the need to serve a full meal. People desire connection much more than they desire a three-course meal. Less is more. And if you lessen your workload, chances are that you will be able to open your door even more!

Look again at the list above. Can you guess what so many of these styles emphasize? *Collaboration!*

Why should the host provide everything? Why does a host need to host in their home? Why must a host be responsible for all of the details? The answer is—they don't have to!

Even if money isn't an obstacle or if you love wearing your chef hat, it's still important for us to collaborate rather than one person taking the reins and running everything. Yes, there is a time and place for that too, but in the regular, slice-of-life socializing, we need to be more about collaboration. More about dividing and conquering—especially when it comes to the planning and spending. Collaboration helps to build a sense of community.

There is always a cost when serving, whether it is your money, time, belongings, or energy. The refreshing news is that you as the host are allowed to find your own individual style and what fits you best. Let your hosting style be one that resonates with you and feels right. Being comfortable with your hosting style and your food and financial choices will help you to more graciously serve your guests.

Your hospitality personality may tend to help or hinder you within the different areas of food and finances. Leaders and Organizers usually zero in on the details and plan well, and this is great! But they will want to make sure to flex and relax when necessary. Entertainers and Includers will want to use their tendencies to help bring the fun and creativity. But they should remember to be responsible with their planning and spending.

Whatever your hospitality personality, work to communicate expectations, create a place for everyone—remember presence trumps presentation—and seek to collaborate!

Do you enjoy the food/menu planning portion of hosting or not so much? Elaborate.

Do you have a budget for hosting and dining out (socially)?

_____

_____

_____

_____

What is one action step you could take with either your food or financial planning that would help you to extend more hospitality?

_____

_____

_____

_____

CHAPTER FIFTEEN

coziness

fanciness and function

I tend to appreciate gatherings that put more emphasis on people than presentation. I have fond memories of meeting in cramped living rooms for youth group meetings with everyone sprawled about, or hosting several young families in our small starter home where, due to limited space, we would naturally overflow to the backyard to make room. These get-togethers flowed well and felt comfortable because there was a relaxed mindset within the group and we were more focused on interacting than on impressing.

When inviting people over to your home, some things can make it challenging for you to fully enjoy having others in your personal space. I want to help you better work through some of these hang-ups. I'll be honest with you: I have them too.

In my survey, more than half of the respondents listed "cleaning" as the part of hosting that they enjoy the least, and the number one hosting reservation shared was the functionality of their home (home design not being a good layout, not enough space, etc.). Our spaces and the pressure for them to feel fancy (whether clean, organized, or decorated) and functional (everything from the floor plan to the parking availability) can unfortunately produce feelings of defeat. We can all too easily feel discouraged before we even attempt to open our front door.

While both of these elements, fanciness and function, can (and sometimes should) have their place, they are not set in stone. These are not essential requirements for you to be a fabulous host. There is a lot of room for how to creatively work within the fancy and functional aspects of hosting. What's most important is that you see your space with a glass-half-full mentality.

You can make any space function well, and with some massaging you can certainly add some sprinkles of fanciness. Realize, however, that whatever your space looks like, whether small and cramped, big and functional, fancy and decorated, or messy and understated, when you welcome others in, you are being generous and vulnerable. Both of those attributes help foster connection and are extensions of your love. I want you to fill up your glass with positivity because your space is just a place. YOU are what makes your house a home.

Fanciness

When we lived overseas, I loved how comfortable and settled our friends and coworkers were in their homes. Typically, the host or hostess had a natural and relaxed style of hosting. And more often than not, they were living in a rental home that was filled with hotel-style furniture. (Furniture that is commonly supplied to embassy and military families.) The furniture was generally neutral-colored, somewhat understated, and definitely more within the realm of what I would call basic home décor. The simple furnishings and styling weren't of high priority or concern for the host and certainly didn't keep them from opening up their home to serve and socialize. While some of the homes were quite lavish in terms of size and amenities, and even sometimes boasted gorgeous outdoor living spaces or pristine pools, none of it really seemed to matter all that much.

I think much of this was due to the reality that as a group of Americans living in a foreign country, we collectively craved community much more than we did curated homes. Rather than a host showing off their home or trying to create a certain "look," the priority was placed on the people in the room rather than on the room itself. There wasn't a focus on being fancy even though some of the homes actually were quite fancy.

By "a focus on being fancy," I mean that the host wasn't overly concerned with having their house in perfect order or their decorating and styling on display. There was more of an emphasis on the festivities. Their homes felt more like "home" because the host was *at home*. Their four walls simply served as a place to graciously welcome others in, and fanciness was not expected or required.

Over the years, we've lived in several older homes. Homes that, if I'm being honest, caused me some angst. Living in our older homes over the years meant that I had to work to accept overly worn carpet, outdated cabinets, and '80s-colored appliances. While this may sound like I'm complaining—and yes, I am a little—it was my reality. I wasn't always proud or comfortable in our homes. I did love each of our older homes, but it was hard for me to not get caught up in the pressure of Pinterest, the HGTV home-improvement inspiration, and yes, my friends' and neighbors' homes. I worked to remind myself that creating a cozy home was much more important to me than creating a perfectly renovated one. I chose to remain grateful and thankful for what each of our homes provided for us rather than focusing too much on what they lacked.

I made an intentional effort to not let the state of our older homes keep me from hosting. Instead, I reminded myself that anyone who cares more about my home and its cleanliness (or lack thereof) than on building relationships probably isn't someone I want to be that close with anyhow. I can tidy up, attempt to make my house clean, and fluff all the pillows, but what I want to do even more is to make my home feel cozy. I've found that sometimes the messes actually add to the level of coziness because they add to the reality that life is being lived! Yes, the dishes in the sink and the shoes piled up by the door can add to a feeling of *home*. These elements can make a space feel lived-in. A (cozy) lived-in house feels more like a home.

There is a spectrum with all things in life. There are people who have more than you (in this case maybe a bigger or cleaner home) and people who have less than you (in this case maybe a more out-dated or smaller home). So with your glass half full, let's focus on viewing your space—whether a shared house with a roommate, your first apartment, a fixer-upper, or your dream home—with contentment.

Contentment entails being comfortable in your space, whatever your space may be. Recognizing all that your home or space can do for you versus what it cannot do. The best and maybe most impor-tant reason to do this is because when you are comfortable, settled, and peace-filled, then your guests will also feel comfortable. This is what my friends modeled for me when we lived overseas. When we went to their homes, I felt at ease in their spaces because they were at ease. I always remind other parents (and myself) that *more is caught than taught*. This same principle applies when you open your door and invite others into your space.

Don't let your home or space limit your hosting opportunities. Make a point to invite others in. People much prefer an invite to an imperfect and well-loved home than not being invited. Create and curate, design and decorate, but do it for YOU so that you can be YOU.

Myquillyn Smith describes the attitude and approach for how to open your home in such a gracious and contented way.

Over time, I've found my method of getting ready for guests is much less focused on my house and how it looks (which is a fancy way of saying I'm less me-focused), and much more focused on my heart and whether I'm in a place to truly listen to, connect with, and be attentive to my guests. This is a strange phenomenon, and it didn't happen overnight. I used to fret over every detail of my house, rearrange vignettes, buy fresh flowers, and try to envision my home from the perspective of a new guest. However, as I focused on creating a place that serves me and others, that represents my family, that I find beautiful, and that isn't overflowing with stuff, I began to think less and less about my house when I had people over. Instead I began to think about the people. And that feels right. You'll know your home is in a good place when you go from thinking about how to make it look better to thinking about how to make it serve better.[1]

Isn't this a beautiful way to think about it? Use your space and shift your focus from "me" to "them." Your cozy space can serve you and serve others well. You get to lead the charge. You don't need to make room for fanciness, but it's always a good idea to make room for comfort and coziness. Both of these elements are great foundations for helping to create close connections.

Like Myquillyn said, *make your home serve better rather than look better.* Then, if you want to sprinkle in a little bit of fanciness, do so—but only if you want to! Serve first, sprinkle second.

Function

The functionality of your space is often the cornerstone of hosting. It's natural to want to be able to offer a seat to everyone, have enough plates, and desire to create an environment where your guests can enjoy themselves and settle in. However, if you live in a space that makes it more challenging for you to have others over, whether because you share your space, find that you stress about your pet(s), don't like the layout of your living/kitchen area, struggle to entertain because you have little kids, or whatever, I get it. You may not be able to change some of the "fixed" portions of your living space right now, but there are some great options that can help to increase the flexibility and functionality of your space. When it comes to functionality, it's important to think outside the box.

One tip is to look at your space after you've hosted and take note of where people congregated and gathered. Look at how things shifted over the course of the event.

- What worked well (food setup, chair placement, coatrack, etc.)?
- Did people move chairs around or pull tables closer?
- What were the common hot spots for conversations?
- Where did people tend *not* to gather?
- What would you do or not do again?

People will make a space functional without even planning to or realizing it! These notes will help you when preparing future get-togethers. While you can't lessen every challenge with your space, you can find ways to work through some of them by being more intentional.

Teamwork

What about asking a friend to cohost with you? Have them help you work on making your space more functional. Maybe rearrange some of your furniture or see if you can borrow some folding chairs. Shuffle things around, see if you can maximize your space and make it work the best for the occasion. Sometimes moving things around can make all the difference!

Or, if you have less room than you desire for the event or number of people, see if you can team up and cohost at a friend's home instead. If someone has a great house with a spacious floor plan or a great outdoor area for entertaining, they may be thrilled that you want to help or take on much of the planning and preparing. Don't be afraid to try new things. If you desire to connect with others you can create the space.

Outside

Could you extend your hosting to an outdoor area? Do you have a community space you could reserve? What about setting up a get-together at a park? There is no need to force the function of your current space if you have some great outdoor options. If the inside of your space is limiting you or if you have specific constraints, then flex and find an option that still allows you to host but that will take the functionality of your space out of the equation. Remember, hosting doesn't have to be in your home. If you are in a season when you don't have the most functional space or adequate time to prepare your space, choosing to host at an outside venue is a fabulous option!

On the Move

Opening your door is a wonderful and welcoming thing to do, especially when it works for you or when you feel called to do so. However, hospitality "on the move" is also a great and doable option. As we've already talked about, every day can be an opportunity to give hospitality away. And when you give hospitality on the move you don't need to pay as much attention to the function of your home (or to making things fancy).

Last week, I took a bouquet of flowers to a member in my fitness class for her birthday. On Valentine's Day, my sweet neighbor delivered gifts to my kids on our doorstep. Then just yesterday, I once again witnessed another example of someone buying someone's order behind them at Starbucks. Small examples of hospitality on the move.

Look at life through your hospitality glasses. Move through your days and weeks, looking for ways to serve others and put others above yourself. Keep the hospitality ripple effect going and going.

My friend Sarah shared this about how she and her roommate use their apartment to serve others.

Within the last year I moved into a new apartment in Colorado. This was my first place of my own and my first opportunity to make my space an extension of myself. The decorating process was my number one priority. I was searching on Pinterest like never before. I was shopping up and down the aisles of HomeGoods any chance I had. I couldn't wait to make my new home a cozy and welcoming environment for all the people I would soon have over. Hosting was never a common practice in my home growing up so I had no idea what it was like to invite friends, acquaintances or even strangers into my home to host them. Going out of state for college I was blessed with friends that invited me into their homes; this is where my eyes were opened for the first time to the idea of "hosting." My friends and their families welcomed me in and made me feel so comfortable.

With the incredibly positive experiences I had in college from people hosting me wonderfully well—I knew I wanted to return the favor to whoever that may be. I knew that wherever I ended up after graduation, hosting was going to be a priority for me. Back to the decorating of my new space—everything was going great until I realized that I would be sharing this space with a roommate I had yet to consult about her views on what our home would be used for. Thankfully she was like-minded in wanting our space to be used in welcoming people and loving on them. My roommate and I are both working for a college organization so we work closely with college-aged students, meaning we get the opportunity to host a lot of dining-hall-going, ramen-noodle-eating, too-much-Red-Bull people. Although their standards are probably lower than the average adult, that doesn't change the excellence in which we should host them. My roommate and I are very similar and very different. This plays into our hosting mindsets as well. If we are cohosting an event we need to celebrate our differences and delegate to our strengths. Having a roommate and hosting can be summed up with the word: *consideration*! I must consider her sleep schedule, her evening routines. I have to be aware of the limitations of our apartment.

Whatever your living situation looks like, if you are all about the fanciness, the layering, and the details, I want to encourage you to carry on because it works for you. If you have a gift when it comes to home décor, then please, decorate until your heart's content! Entertainers and Includers, these are usually some of your natural strengths, so play to them! Leaders and Organizers, you are likely to have a keen attention to details, which can help with maximizing the functionality of a space.

Most of all, remember to relax when it comes to the pressure you put on yourself. While it's nice to tidy and straighten things up before hosting, realize that when others see some of the mess, like backpacks in the entryway or piles of things that need to go back upstairs, this actually brings a sense of coziness. It shows life. So let some of the lived-in show—it's so worth it!

> Practice being present over the presentation.

Fanciness and function have their place but remember that people should always come first! Practice being present over the presentation.

How do you feel about your current living situation? Specifically when it comes to hosting, are you happy with how it functions? Why or why not?

Do you like your level of fanciness (your home décor, organization, and/or style)? Are YOU comfortable in your home?

_____

_____

_____

What could you do to make your home or space serve you and others better?

_____

_____

_____

your hospitality help

People will forget what you said.
They will forget what you did.
But they will never forget
how you made them feel.

Maya Angelou

CHAPTER SIXTEEN

hosting tips

how-to

This last section of the book is designed to be a practical resource for you as you embark on hosting with a fresh perspective. To help you with the various ups and downs of hospitality, specifically the methods, manners, and mission, I have included some hosting tips and themes. The contributors to this section are women who bring different experiences and backgrounds, and their own hospitality personalities. My hope is that you will find yourself referring to these chapters often and gain more answers to your hospitality questions.

The following hosting tips are brought to you by my hosting team (I just made that up): Bri Totman (an Includer and a native-born Midwesterner now living in adventurous Colorado), Janet Campbell (an Includer, my beautiful mom, an empty nester and hostess extraordinaire), Inger Binns (an Organizer, my dear friend who exemplifies why we should never take life or hosting too seriously), Haley Pearson (an Includer, my youngest sister, and the most relaxed hostess I know—who also happens to make the best guacamole this side of Texas), Jill Beadles (an Includer, my tennis partner for life, who has effortlessly hosted diplomats from all over the world), Julie Pitts (an Entertainer, my favorite coworker, who models how to host as a single person and love others really well), and Tammy Tank (an Includer, who shares graciously how to receive hospitality from others when you need it the most. She knows firsthand what it means to walk through a personal crisis).

Tips from Includer Bri Totman

Hosting with Roommates

1. Show consideration in a big way! I was really awed by my roommate recently. Before hosting overnight stays for several people within a week, she made sure to consider me. Not only did she ask beforehand whether it would be OK to have guests, she later reiterated that her checking in wasn't to check off a box. She really wanted to know if it was OK. Does this situation work for me—really; if not, she wanted me to share honest thoughts and feelings about it. Her consideration wasn't standard, it was above and beyond, the type that flows from a heart that chooses to humbly love and consider others' interests.

2. Make thoughtful communication a must. My roommate and I both have at times prayerfully approached communication and waited to talk in person instead of text, or waited on sending a text message until the time seemed right (not in the emotional heat of the moment, I mean). That has been a lifesaver. It has made for healthy conversations, allowing us to get on the same page in preparation for hosting. Never underestimate the importance of timing with communication.

3. Plan and organize what you can and then go with the flow. Whether you are choosing to host together or separately, have a loose, communicated plan in mind to execute.

We've talked about food, cleaning, and space for shared hosting, as well as the use of space when she had overnight guests—only one bathroom here, folks! A little planning can go a long way in alleviating unnecessary stress.

4. If you are planners or want to be, might I suggest a calendar? We have a joint wall calendar hanging in our cute kitchen. Best thing ever. We both are able to jot down schedules and events, keeping mostly ourselves and each other in the know.

5. Let your home be their home too. This might be obvious, but I (we) love making people feel truly welcome—the "our home is your home" type of welcome. Make sure to check in with your roommate though, about any off-limit items. Respectful boundaries are a good thing.

Tips from Includer Janet Campbell

Dinner Parties, Open Houses, Appetizers and Wine

1. Best number for a dinner party is six to eight. More than that, and the talkers tell stories while the quiet ones fade into the background.

2. Inviting two couples you know who don't know each other but have commonality is a nice way to spread friendships. What's the purpose of hosting anyway? I believe it's for sharing around the table and growing our social connections.

3. How often to invite people in? Once this is determined, get it on the calendar! Once the people and date are chosen, you're committed! (This can be the hardest part.) Hosting gets easier with experience.

4. Let them bring food—ALWAYS. By doing so, it feels more like hospitality than entertaining and everyone gets some

praise for their efforts. I usually ask them to bring appetizers or bread or dessert, while I do the main, sides, and so on. Feel free to buy prepared food for part of the dinner! Don't let the "food" part keep you from opening your home. When a guest says, "What can I do?" let them toss the salad, make the guacamole, fill the water glasses, and so on.

5. I love simple yet delicious food, most of which can be prepared ahead. For a large crowd, apps and wine are a hit. Everyone brings an appetizer to share and the host does the beverages (be sure to have a nonalcoholic option).

6. Table setting: We have inherited china, silver flatware, and crystal that I like using, but I don't use it all *together*. For example, I will use silver flatware with everyday plates. I like to keep the rest of the table simple but appealing. A centerpiece can be simple flowers or candles. Children especially love place cards. I like to use cloth napkins, but even they are casual—some are vintage and shabby. A pretty table is visually pleasing, and I think it's a way to make people feel special. I also get the nicer paper napkins for guests.

7. Games: Though there can be reluctance, we usually break the ice with games. This never fails to bring a group together, in our experience. We have a box of cards on the table with questions. To make it nonthreatening, the guest can look through the cards until they find one they want to answer, then they can just answer it or the whole table does. We also love Catch Phrase: quick to learn, lots of laughs, and everyone gets to know each other better. For large groups, Pictionary on an easel is fun.

8. Cleanup: Do they help with the dishes? It depends. Some guests will insist on it; sometimes when I am a guest they insist I DO NOT. We like to quickly stash the dishes in the

sink and do them later after the group has left as we process the event. This is an area to be flexible in.

9. Host gifts: This can be tricky. Someone who always brings one puts pressure on you to do the same. I think they are nice but can become a burden. Perhaps they are most appropriate when you are staying overnight with someone? I do try to keep a few on hand to take to people (things like small candles or a bottle of wine).

Overnight Guests

1. Make people feel welcome. Greet them with a smile and show them where to put their bags.

2. A good guest room can be found with these thoughtful items: luggage racks (or somewhere else to put bags), nice sheets, extra pillows and blankets, a night-light, reading lamps.

3. For the bathroom it's thoughtful to have nice towels and a mat, disposable cups, cotton balls, Q-tips, toothpaste, packaged toothbrushes (many times mine have been needed), shampoo, and washcloths. Some folks don't like liquid bath soap, so I keep nicer packaged hotel soap bars handy.

4. Things to be aware of or sensitive to: the temperature of your house (ask your guests if they are comfortable or need anything), a bonging clock (we have one that we don't hear but that keeps guests awake, so we turn it off).

5. What will you be doing while you're together? Some discussion ahead of time is a good idea. We like to make a list of options and go over it together. Getting a group of guests out the door to do something can be difficult. Extra patience may be needed; remember why you invited them!

Being a Guest

1. Be thankful!

2. Bring a small gift for the host, such as a jar of homemade jam, cocktail napkins, or a small plant.

3. Compliment the cook.

4. Be aware of ways you can help by picking up after yourself, giving your hosts some time alone, pitching in, and so on.

5. Strip the sheets and take them along with towels to the laundry room when leaving unless otherwise instructed.

6. Reciprocate: invite your hosts to visit you or meet for a meal.

Tips from Organizer Inger Binns

Keep It Fun and Cozy

1. The things that I treasure, remember, and enjoy the most are when they feel like Grandma's house, or just feel comfortable. One of my favorite times was when we went to Morgan's house; we wore pajamas, ate pancakes, and just laughed and had the best time! Our lives are so overscheduled and we're always on the go. At the end of the day, the last thing I want to do is make small talk, have to put my best foot forward, or worry about how things will go that evening. I like when you can just go be yourself and the evening is kind of a refuge from the busyness of life.

2. Some of our best dinners have been these scrambled-up, ridiculous times. I kid you not, every single time I have someone over for dinner, a portion of the meal is an absolute disaster! Something's ruined every time. And I think I've come to expect it and it makes me laugh—it's funny. I

just hope that it's never the main component of the meal. I really like the humanity of casual dinners. I don't ever want people to show up at my house with hostess gifts. I don't ever want people to show up dressing super nice (although I have very strong opinions against tank tops at the dinner table). And proper table manners are a must. You can wear pajamas to dinner, but you'd better hold your fork correctly.

3. One of my favorite stories is one my husband shared with me while we were living in Japan. I had gone back to the US with our two little girls, and my husband was invited over to a Sunday dinner at our dear friend's home. Well, the host had completely forgotten about the invite but told him to still come over anyway. She was totally unprepared and hadn't been grocery shopping, so all she had on hand was a blueberry muffin mix, some Doritos, and spaghetti. So that's what she served! We still talk about it, and it is one of our fondest and most cherished memories. I just like the idea of simple, family fun and very, very informal.

Tips from Includer Haley Pearson

Entertaining in Your Home

1. Don't let not having the "perfect" entertaining space hold you back from hosting. We have hosted potluck dinners in a 3800-square-foot house and in a 1300-square-foot house with no backyard. Bottom line—people are just happy to be invited. If you focus on the time together with people, it doesn't matter if you hate your couch or think your living room is too small. Try it out and see how it goes! If it gets crowded, walk to a nearby park together or suggest an after-dinner trip to a nearby ice cream shop.

2. Similarly, don't wait until your house is perfectly clean. I have heard so many times that people waited to host until they had their cleaning service come. (Is it just me or does everyone have a cleaning service? I have had a cleaner zero days of my life, and I'm pretty sure my house reflects that.) We are not trying to impress our friends. Of course you want things picked up, but walking into a spotless house can actually make guests feel uncomfortable—too perfect can feel stiff, especially when kids are involved.

3. It can feel so vulnerable to bring people into our homes. But I believe that's where we truly connect, and we should do that just as we are, not as an image of what we'd like to be. If you truly don't love hosting at your house, you can still initiate a group gathering. Suggest a bring-your-own picnic dinner at a park or meet friends at a pizza parlor for dinner. The point is to connect and initiate a plan, even if you don't want to have everyone over.

Kids—Socializing and Simplifying

1. I love nothing more than a houseful of kiddos playing and bonding together. If you're having several families over, it can help to set some ground rules (e.g., shoes off, no food in certain rooms, toys need to stay upstairs, etc.). If you set expectations ahead of time it will make cleanup easier and keep everyone on the same page. Also, feed the kids separately. Often we will feed the kids first so the adults can sit down and enjoy a longer meal at the table.

2. Give yourself permission to use paper plates. Keeping cleanup simple makes you more likely to focus on connecting with people rather than doing dishes.

3. Put out a pen so guests can label their drinks. If you're using disposable cups, put out a Sharpie. They also make markers for glasses that wash off in the dishwasher.

4. I always keep a few gluten-free and nut-free (common food allergies) snack things at my house. A lot of people have food allergies/sensitivities, and I like to have a box of, say, gluten-free crackers to offer.

Traditions

1. Start some simple traditions. We began throwing an annual Christmas cookie–decorating party and invite several of our friends to come with their kids. It has become something we all look forward to, and it couldn't be simpler. People bring appetizer-type food to graze on and sugar cookies to decorate, and I cover our dining room table with various (store-bought) frostings and sprinkles. I use a big sheet of Christmas wrapping paper as a tablecloth and put on a Christmas movie. Last year, we printed out song lyrics and went caroling as a group to a retirement home. Most people I talk with find holidays so stressful, and having time carved out for friends—or chosen family—eases up the tension and gets us in the holiday spirit.

2. We also rotate regularly on Sundays in the fall to watch football together. I am actually a big football fan now, and I used to just show up for the food and company. You can order a few pizzas and grab some beer and you have a party.

3. Last Cinco de Mayo, we had an impromptu barbeque. I bought a $10 piñata and some candy the day of, and the kids thought it was the best thing ever. Dare to be spontaneous, and don't be afraid to order food in or buy prepared food from the grocery store.

Tips from Includer Jill Beadles

Hosting and Menu Planning

1. Plan your menu at least a couple of days ahead. Make a shopping list and plan to buy the ingredients at least a day ahead of time.

2. Stick with meals you are familiar with. Don't try to make beef bourguignon just to try to impress your guests (make it if you know it well). If you want to try something new, try it out on your family a few days before. Way less stress if it doesn't go well—and easy to order pizza with your loved ones.

3. When we entertained a lot, we had different guests all the time. Typically, we served the same two menus—ones that I could easily manage and knew well. You don't need to reinvent the wheel every time you have people over.

4. Keep it simple. Simple food, simple ingredients. Also use ingredients you are familiar with.

5. Make as much ahead of time as possible. This allows you to minimize kitchen time and maximize socializing time. Toss the salad beforehand and add the dressing right before serving. Have all ingredients measured out if you have to make something right before you eat. Make everything in the sauce and just heat it up before serving. We used to make prime rib—I had a recipe where it was all done before dinner—that worked every time (Chef John's Perfect Prime Rib). Our dog did eat it once while it was on the counter—but that's another story.

6. Make lists of everything (and I mean everything you need to do). Have you watched Top Chef? This is what lots of them do on their prep and cooking days—no detail is omitted. This also makes it easy when someone asks if they can help—you can easily look at your list

and give a task, without having to think about what else you have to do.

7. Keep a list of who came to dinner and what you served. This may not be an issue for you, but when we entertained frequently, I could not remember who ate what and when.

8. Clean as you go. You will be much happier at the end of the night.

9. Overall, relax and enjoy your guests. Your guests are happy to see you and are happy someone else is cooking!

Tips from Entertainer Julie Pitts

During my single years, I've enjoyed hosting various events in my home, but the two most frequent events I've hosted have been small group Bible or book studies and an annual Christmas party. I never imagined I would still be single at forty-two years old, but it's a season of life that can bless others if you allow it to. Single people have time and energy to focus on serving others that people with families often don't. Leading small groups in my home has been a blessing to me and others, and it brings me joy to see women growing in their faith. Throwing an annual Christmas party has been my way of "merging" my work world with my church and social world. I am able to spend my favorite holiday, Christmas, with the people in my life who feel like family. I often have one hundred–plus people at my Christmas party, and many of them have told me they look forward to seeing each other at my party each year.

Small Group Bible/Book Studies

1. The size of the group is important; six to eight is ideal to encourage sharing between participants. Less than six may make participants feel pressured to share (especially early

on), and more than ten doesn't allow for sharing to happen between the whole group.

2. Consider the topic/authors and who would benefit most when you're deciding who to invite to be part of the group.

3. Arrange furniture (chairs/sofas) to foster a feeling of inclusiveness and to encourage sharing. I arrange mine in a circle in my home so that everyone has eye contact with group members.

4. Start out with social time if a goal is to build relationships. I start my book studies with thirty minutes of social time and always serve a light snack/dessert and beverages such as hot tea and water. Chocolate-dipped strawberries are a favorite and are easy to make the day of and then stick in the fridge. For a group of ten or less people, I serve out of real mugs and on everyday china with real silverware.

5. Have the first meeting begin with introductions (have questions prepared for members to answer in front of the group), an ice-breaker activity, a discussion of what the books are, and an outline of what will be read when. Conclude with a few minutes for members to ask questions.

6. Be overprepared with materials (better to have too many handouts than not enough). Have extra pens/pencils and something for them to write on.

7. Stick to the time schedule. Try to start at the designated time and always end on time to foster respect for participants' home lives.

8. Consider limiting each person's verbal responses so everyone has time to share. (Decide ahead of time what the cut-off time is and make this clear to the group.)

9. Conclude the study with an evening for members to share highlights and "gold nuggets" they received from the study. Consider how to wrap up the small group time in a creative and meaningful way.

Hosting an Annual Christmas Party

1. Determine how many people you can host, and arrange to move furniture for the desired party size. I usually have fifty to one hundred people stop by, so I clean out my garage and set up two extra food tables there. I use a space heater to warm up the garage and place about twelve small folding chairs in there so people can choose to sit or stand. I also have overflow seating in my loft upstairs with a small table of food and overflow seating in the basement. Having the food spread out in different rooms helps keep people from congregating in only one area.

2. I use Evite for RSVPs, which notifies me as people reply and saves the email addresses so they can be used from year to year.

3. Plan the menu well in advance. I usually have a friend or caterer make the appetizers since these have to be made closer to the party date, and I prepare all of the desserts since they can be made a few days in advance. Plan out the baking schedule and spread out recipes to keep it from being overwhelming. I also make small-portion desserts so people can try several things.

4. Make sure to include a variety of beverages, alcoholic and nonalcoholic. Have a designated station for each beverage type. I place all of the wine in my dining room on my wine console; beer, soda, and bottled waters in my garage in large ice-filled tubs; and hot cider in my kitchen in Crock-Pots.

5. For larger parties, Christmas-themed plates and napkins work well. I use plastic cups for wine and put Christmas stickers on them (different stickers) to help people keep track of their cup. I also try to stick with finger food that doesn't require silverware (toothpicks are a great option to place on tables).

6. Make a master list of ingredients needed for recipes, and make one trip to the store to get what's needed about one week before the party.

7. Employ friends to help with party setup the day of and teardown if possible.

8. Don't light candles if children are coming. Have carpet stain removers available in case of spilled wine. Have extra trash cans set up in different rooms, and clearly label a large trash can and recycling bin.

9. Lights and music make a Christmas party extra festive. I hang lights up in my garage and put small strands of lights in different rooms inside. Consider playing a mix of Christmas music as background music (I create a big playlist on an old iPhone), or hire a musician. I once hired a band to play in my garage and another time hired a violinist to play in my loft.

10. Explain parking availability on the invitation, and try to clear an ice-free path to the house if conditions are snowy.

11. Many people will bring coats and purses. Clear off multiple beds if possible and ask people to place coats/purses in bedrooms.

12. Dress up as much as you'd like, but make sure your attire is comfortable for several hours and that you can move about easily.

13. Make a to-do list for each day of the week leading up to the party to stay on track and to keep preparation from becoming overwhelming.

14. Eat a small plate of food prior to the party, and try to stay relaxed and have fun!

15. Above all, enjoy your guests and their presence, and watch new relationships form as your worlds merge for one special evening a year.

Tips from Includer Tammy Tank

Giving in Times of Need

1. Practical ideas: deliver everyday paper products (paper plates, cups, napkins, etc.), bring a meal on a holiday, offer to decorate for the holidays, or drop off basic grocery items.

2. Ask how you can help, but even better, offer options. Examples: Can I take your child to and from school? May I mow your lawn every Saturday? What do you like on your hamburgers? (This communicates that you want to bring a meal, you just need to know what to include on their hamburgers; this is a specific and clear offering.)

3. Continue to invite those who are going through a crisis to your gatherings. Even if they can't make it, they still want to feel included.

4. Don't be afraid of saying the wrong thing. Admit you don't know what to say, but do say that you want to be there for them.

5. When you communicate good wishes to someone in a crisis, consider not asking them questions but rather giving them an "out" on even responding or acknowledging your outreach. I had people text and say they don't expect to receive a reply, or no reply needed. It was nice to take the pressure off.

6. Don't take it personally if the person you are serving seems tired or unresponsive; it's not personal. When our friend came over to put up our Christmas tree, my husband, Tim, sat down on the couch and started to ask him how his day was going. Our friend said to him, "You don't need to visit with me. I'm not here to visit with you." This was nice because it gave Tim an "out" on using his energy.

7. Text or email a sick person directly rather than their caregivers. (A few people did this regularly, and I thought it was nice because my husband could read their messages when he was truly able to versus me having to weed through the communication.)

Receiving in Times of Need

1. Remember, it's OK to let people help you.
2. Receiving help can feel hard, but remember you can and will be able to pay it forward in a later life season.
3. Consider assigning committee heads to each area of help needed (meals, yard care, childcare, rides, etc.). It will benefit you to have someone else coordinating communication in specific areas, because you may be receiving a lot of communication from people who simply care, and it's hard to weed though so much communication from various sources.
4. Create a front door sign that communicates visiting hours, and include a journal for visitors to leave notes or instructions.
5. Let go and let others organize the different forms of help you need.

CHAPTER SEVENTEEN

hosting themes

diy

I asked some amazing hostesses to share their tried-and-true hosting themes with you. These women live all across the country and are in unique and different life seasons. I hope you enjoy their hosting themes and find that they prompt you to plan your next gathering. These are examples of how to "do it yourself." Hosting does not need to be complicated. Cheers!

Donut Brunch

Hostess Kimbra Naber, an Includer, is a momma living in Indianapolis with two little rascals. Her daughter gives her a run for her money, and her son knows how to cuddle all the stress out of her life. Fun fact: both of her kiddos were born overseas while she and her husband were living in Kuala Lumpur, Malaysia. Organizing is her passion and she is dedicated to helping people create a space to enjoy their journeys (www.reorgproject.com). Travel is another passion of hers. She loves to experience other cultures and bring old and new friends together. She likes to keep things simple when entertaining so that the focus is on the fellowship.

Theme: Donut Brunch! Adults and kids alike love this theme. I've used it for children's birthday parties and midmorning sporting events. Everyone loves to indulge once in a while, and this is such an easy yet decadent way to do so!

Decorations: This part is so easy. Let the donuts be the star of the show! I love using small and large cake stands as well as various-size platters to house the donuts and donut holes. Regardless of what or who this is for, there are tons of donut-style decorations out there. I usually just add some colorful balloons and vases of fresh flowers. Easy is the name of the game here, so disposable tablecloths, plates, cutlery, and cups are the way to go. I even encourage guests to come in comfy clothes and pajamas!

Entertainment: Play a game to guess how many donut holes are in a bowl/jar. Draw names and let someone else pick your donut! Buy a huge inflatable pool donut and use it not only for decoration but also for a game of throwing donut holes through it (outside of the house, of course!).

Menu: This is such a fun yet easy menu! Picking up donuts and donut holes from your favorite local spot is easy. Adding in some simple fruit trays or skewers keeps things simple. An overnight egg casserole is a great complement. Make sure you cut the casserole into smaller bites so a little goes a long way! For beverages, make it fun. A coffee bar, some mimosas, and a childhood favorite—Orange Julius! A small glass is the perfect amount with a straw for ease. Have a blast with this theme—there are no wrong ways!

Beverages

- Coffee bar
- Mimosas
- Orange Julius

Main Dish

- Donuts
- Overnight egg casserole
- Fruit trays/skewers

Recipes

OVERNIGHT EGG CASSEROLE

Ingredients

10	eggs, lightly beaten
12 slices	of cooked bacon, chopped
3 c.	milk
	salt and pepper
2 c.	shredded cheese blend
12 slices	of bread, cubed
1 c.	veggies, chopped (mushrooms, peppers, etc.)

Instructions

Coat a 9x13 baking dish with nonstick spray.

In a large bowl, whisk together eggs, bacon, milk, salt, and pepper.

Layer half of the cubed bread, cheese, and veggies in the baking dish. Repeat with remaining bread, cheese, and veggies.

Top with egg mixture.

Cover and refrigerate overnight.

Bake at 325 degrees for 50–60 minutes, until eggs are set. Makes 12 small/medium servings.

HOMEMADE ORANGE JULIUS

Ingredients

1	12 oz. container frozen orange juice concentrate
2 c.	vanilla yogurt

173

> 2 c.   milk
> 1–2 c.   ice cubes
>
> Instructions
>
> Place all ingredients, except ice cubes, in blender and blend on high, adding ice cubes slowly, until frothy. Makes 6–8 small glasses.

Platter Party

Hostess Kate Merrick, an Entertainer, is a California-based home-schooling surf mom, author, and church planter living with a huge-bearded husband, a ravenous teenage son, and a six-year-old daughter. She loves throwing outdoor dinner parties with gorgeous table arrangements (usually some greens foraged from her yard), but it's always on the simple side. She believes that all you need is food and love (and a great soundtrack)! Visit her at www .kmerrick.com.

Theme: Platter Party—or you could call it Charcuterie if you're feeling hip. This is easy, gorgeous, fun, and can be done at the drop of a hat. I love the comfortable feel of laughter and crowding around a beautiful wood board spilling over with yummy food, and it works as a laid-back but lovely evening for old friends, girlfriends, or even new friends. It can really go in any direction, but I'll share the things I always have on hand that you can throw together an hour before guests arrive.

Decorations: I love decorating with edible flowers and herbs. I grow rosemary and have clippings of it scattered throughout the savory boards as well as pansies scattered over the veggies and fruits. Thrift store wine goblets add a funky/elegant look and can be filled with herbs, flowers, or even nut mixes or olives. Mismatched pretty plates from the thrift store spread across the table make it colorful, feminine, and quirky. Copious amounts of candles and a great jazzy playlist transform it into something special.

Entertainment: We love making a playlist with each guest choosing a song. We keep it secret as we make it, and when each guest's fave song plays, there's lots of hooting and sometimes some dancing! Or play Would You Rather. This keeps the conversation going for hours! I have a set of question cards, but you can make up your own.

Menu:

Beverages

- "Mocktails" (sparkling water with any juice and a splash of bitters) garnished with lavender or fruit
- Prosecco or Pellegrino with a spritz of any citrus and garnished with lavender
- Any great wine—red, white, or rosé, depending on time of year

Main Dish—the Platters!

- Summer sausage with various mustards (blue cheese mustard or honey mustard). Salami goes great with medium-hard cheeses like a sharp cheddar or pecorino.
- Soft cheese like Brie goes great either baked to softness or at room temperature served with apricot or fig jam on top.
- Fresh figs taste amazing with a dollop of goat cheese and honey.
- Prosciutto can be wrapped around melon slices, dates, or asparagus (either baked or blanched) and stacked up like logs.
- Soft, mild cheeses such as mascarpone or even crème fraîche are great with fresh berries.

- Anything pickled (caper berries, artichokes, cornichons, asparagus, olives), fresh fruits in season scattered with herbs, dates, cut-up veggies surrounding bowls of dips, crackers, a hot baguette, focaccia, even frozen pizza will work. When they are piled up together with nuts and rosemary sprigs sprinkled around, the look is really elegant.

Dessert

- This can be in the same style of the platters: broken piles of chocolate bars with nut butters to dip; marshmallows, M&Ms, and coconut flakes to sprinkle on top. Graham crackers or other cookies work well too. Just make sure it's piled up in a loose but aesthetically pleasing formation on a great wood platter, and everyone loves it. No recipes here, folks!

Helpful Hint: *Stock up on jars of artichokes, different types of olives, dates, nuts, cured meats, and crackers, and you will never be at a loss for what to feed your people. These things keep a long time. Add cheeses that you love that keep if unopened in the refrigerator. You can pour honey over them or sprinkle them with herbs and flowers growing outside your window and you have an instant Platter Party!*

Toast Bar

Hostess Julie Chambless, an Includer, is a single fortysomething schoolteacher and fitness instructor in Southern California. In San Diego, people are all about eating out, trying new restaurants, and spending an afternoon eating and drinking in the sun. And yes, the stereotypes are true . . . almost everyone has a food "thing"—dairy-free, gluten-free, nut-free, vegan, vegetarian, Paleo, Keto, and so on.

Theme: Toast Bar! This theme is a fun take on the popular avocado toast and covers sweet, savory, and every type of food issue out there. It is easy to take care of any size of group.

Decorations: The great thing about this theme is that the food is so colorful with so much texture that it makes the place look great without decorations. You can easily switch it up with whatever your crowd happens to be. For a baby shower, simply add your theme. For a lady's brunch, a few hydrangeas, some light ribbon or lace to tie around, and you are set.

Entertainment: Phones in a basket labeled "Be with the people you are with"! Funny how easily conversation happens when no one has their phone to depend on. Ask people ahead for their favorite song for a fun playlist. People can guess who chose each song.

Menu: Make-it-yourself is always a fun and easy way to keep people talking and trying new things while staying away from foods they dislike or can't have without it becoming awkward.

Beverages

- Lemonade in pretty bottles or glass carafes
- A selection of juices and Prosecco or champagne to create different mimosas
- Fruit-infused water (definitely adds color and a pretty touch to the table)

Main Dish

- Toast! Be sure you have a couple of toasters handy. Get a variety of breads to spice up the fun and flavors of the toast and to serve everyone's needs.
- Nut butter and non-peanut options such as almond or cashew butter

- Pesto
- Ricotta with honey
- Goat cheese
- Tomatoes
- Arugula
- Cucumbers
- Avocado
- Bacon
- Smoked salmon
- Salt, pepper, red pepper flakes, Everything but the Bagel seasoning (from Trader Joe's)

Southern Afternoon Tea

Hostess Julie Davis, an Includer, is a working mom with a husband and three kids (two teen boys and one little girl) who lives in Texas. The Davises live busy lives, but every once in a while, Julie likes to come home early and set up an afternoon tea for her favorite people. Her kids love coming home from school to a table full of treats! She tries to do this when her husband can be home a little earlier from work too. If she serves a meal, she often makes an Asian coleslaw with rotisserie chicken; then they have the tea after the salad. It's not exactly an afternoon tea at that point, but sometimes it's fun to break the rules!

Theme: An afternoon tea is so simple, yet so few people have ever experienced one. I keep mine on the "simpler is better" side, but feel free to go all out if you want. I have had a tea for my girlfriends, a planning committee, neighbors I want to get to know, and my family.

Decorations: I serve afternoon tea using my wedding china. I know, I know! But I like bringing it out more than once a year. If you don't have any china, look around at garage sales or thrift stores for cute cups, saucers, and salad plates. I also bring out a nice tablecloth and some of my nicer serving trays and tiered trays. Feel free to use paper plates too! The whole point is to make a nice spread for your friends and family so they can sit down, enjoy some special treats, and spend time together.

Entertainment: Lots of conversation starters! For example: Would you really want to be royalty? Why or why not? If you won the lottery, where would you want to go on vacation? Tell us the best thing that happened today/this week. What's been the worst or most embarrassing thing?

- Table Questions: Sometimes I type up some questions on card stock and cut them out. (You can also handwrite questions on index cards.) I leave these on the table in front of each place setting. Each guest takes a turn reading the questions. As the host, I try to pay attention to the answers and follow up with more questions to keep the conversation going. I also make sure that each person gets a turn to answer.
- Host Facilitator: As an alternative, I think of topics and questions ahead of time to keep the conversation going. I toss these questions to the group when there is a quiet moment, always making sure to grab on to details that can lead to other discussions or entertaining anecdotes.
- Guessing Game: It's also fun to make a few different types of tea ahead of time and have your guests guess the flavors.

Menu:

Beverages

- Lots of different types of teas to choose from (Earl Grey, English Breakfast, Lemon Zinger, Peach, Chamomile, Peppermint, Sleepytime), cream, honey, and sugar

179

lumps. You can find sugar lumps in the grocery store. These always bring a smile!

- Lemonade as an option, if desired.

Treats / Main Dish

- Finger sandwiches cut into small triangles or squares, scones, muffins, cookies, mini cupcakes, lemon curd (Trader Joe's has my fave!), fresh fruit with Fluffy Cream. There are lots of recipes for these treats online, or use your grandmother's recipe, which will add to the conversation. In a hurry? Check out the bakery at your local grocery store.
- Luncheon or early dinner: make an Asian coleslaw with rotisserie chicken to serve if you want a heartier meal.

Recipes

ASIAN COLESLAW

Ingredients

Salad

1 bag	of ramen noodles, Oriental flavor
1 Tbsp.	butter
1 Tbsp.	olive oil
1 c.	of pecans or almonds, chopped
1 bag	of coleslaw
1 bunch	of green onions, chopped

Dressing

3 Tbsp.	vinegar
3 Tbsp.	sugar
	flavor packet from ramen noodles
½ c.	vegetable oil

Instructions

Salad: Break up the ramen noodles into small pieces. Heat a sauté pan on medium. Add butter and olive oil. Add the nuts and broken noodles to the pan. Sauté until golden brown. Remove from heat and cool.

In a large bowl, mix the coleslaw with the green onions. Toss the salad with the dressing. Add the nuts and ramen noodles and toss. Serve immediately. (Really! This salad needs to be served right after mixing as the noodles get soggy.)

If you want to add protein, cut up a rotisserie chicken and add to the top. Serves 4–6.

Dressing: Add vinegar, sugar, and ramen flavor packet to a bowl and mix until blended. With a whisk or fork, slowly add vegetable oil.

FLUFFY CREAM

Ingredients

1	8 oz. block of cream cheese, softened
1 jar	of marshmallow cream
1	container of Cool Whip

Instructions

Combine cream cheese and marshmallow cream using a mixer until fluffy. Fold in the Cool Whip. Refrigerate several hours before serving.

Serve on top of fresh fruit like strawberries, grapes, and apples. This can also be served on the side as a dip.

Mediterranean Nights

Hostess Krista Gilbert, an Includer, is a Pacific Northwest mountain girl who loves people, life stories, Jesus, family, sunsets on the northern lakes, skiing fast, and lipstick. You know, the essentials. She lives with her husband of twenty-three years, Erik, and their four kids. She lives by the truth that love changes us and heals us, and often that love is rooted in gathering at the table. It's that important. You can find her talking about all of these things on her podcast, *The Open Door Sisterhood*, or at www.kristagilbert.com.

Theme: Mediterranean Nights, Opa! This is a festive theme that brings the energy and lighthearted fun of the Greeks to your table. Works very well for large groups. A total crowd pleaser! (For additional Greek recipes, Ina Garten is a great resource.)

Decorations: Think about the landscape of Greece. White buildings against blue skies, wispy magenta flowers growing up around doorways, wood structures combined with iron crosses and turquoise accents. Use these same elements. Begin with white tablecloths, then build your theme with wooden boxes, simple iron décor, and brightly colored flowers (real or faux). Be sure to add greenery to the table in the form of succulents or a topiary.

Entertainment: Mediterranean music is a must. Find premade playlists on Spotify or Pandora, or make your own! Greeks love to dance. Teach everyone Greek dances like the sirtaki or the hasapiko. Most of these dances are performed side by side with arms linked, which makes it even more fun! Invite everyone to give a toast at the table, and instead of saying cheers, give a hearty "Opa!" This is a word Greeks use at celebrations.

Menu:

Appetizer

- Goat cheese log with lemon and thyme served with grilled rosemary flatbread

Beverages

- Water (with mint sprigs, lemon slices, or cucumber)
- Wines—Shiraz, Riesling, Pinot Gris, or light Moscato

Main Dish

- Greek Chicken (I use the Greek Chicken marinade recipe on carlsbadcravings.com)
- Lamb kebabs

Sides

- Hummus (I use Ina Garten's hummus recipe), Greek salad, grilled pita bread, tzatziki, baba ghanoush, rosemary sprigs, lemon wedges, kalamata olives, feta crumbles, sliced cucumbers, sundried tomatoes

Dessert

- Baklava, of course!

Lettuce Wrap Bar

Hostesses April Huard, an Organizer, and Abby Miller, an Includer, are sisters living near Ann Arbor, Michigan, who love to cook for fun. They hold various day jobs and are busy moms (eight kids between the two of them), so their style of cooking is simple. They both love to cook fresh meals that can be put on the table every day of the week for family, friends, and neighbors. The sisters share their love of cooking on their blog at www.everydaytable.org.

Theme: Lettuce Wrap Bar. This theme works well with both small and large groups. It's ideal for a family gathering, girls' night, book club, hosting new neighbors, and so on. A lettuce wrap bar is also perfect for meeting dietary needs and preferences; each guest can build their own wrap exactly the way they want it!

Decorations: Spread white butcher paper on the buffet table. Use a black marker to label the various toppings right on the paper—this is visually pleasing and so simple! Fill in with bright, fresh flowers. Be sure to supply small bowls for the dipping sauce. The dessert can also double as a beautiful centerpiece; arrange chocolates and berries on a board or platter for guests to sample.

Entertainment: Depending on the occasion, ask guests to go around the table and share about a book they're reading, their favorite road trip, or something that they've learned lately. The goal is to enjoy nourishing food while also nourishing souls!

Menu:

Appetizers

- Edamame cooked and served in the shell and salted
- Fresh pineapple

Beverages

- Mojitos
- Lemonade
- Sparkling water
- White wine—Riesling, Pinot Grigio, or Moscato

Main Dish

- Lettuce cups (butter lettuce works best)
- Meat filling (recipe below)
- Steamed white basmati or jasmine rice
- Toppings:

Chopped peanuts

Shredded carrots

Chopped green onion

Thinly sliced radishes

Bean sprouts

Thinly sliced cucumbers

Sesame seeds

Dipping sauce (recipe below)

Dessert

- Selection of chocolates and berries (dark chocolate, raspberries, truffles, chocolate-covered nuts, etc.)

Recipes

LETTUCE WRAP MEAT FILLING

Ingredients

2 lbs.	ground beef or turkey
2 Tbsp.	sesame oil
4	garlic cloves, minced
½ c.	brown sugar
½ c.	soy sauce
1½ tsp.	fresh ginger, minced
	salt and pepper
1½ tsp.	crushed red pepper (optional)

Instructions

Heat large skillet over medium heat. Brown ground beef or turkey, drain fat, and add sesame oil and garlic.

Add brown sugar, soy sauce, ginger, salt and pepper, and red pepper (if using) to the meat. Simmer for 5–10 minutes, allowing flavors to combine. Serves 6.

LETTUCE WRAP DIPPING SAUCE

Ingredients

½ c.	soy sauce
¼ c.	rice wine vinegar
1 Tbsp.	brown sugar
2	garlic cloves, minced
1 tsp.	sesame oil

Instructions

Whisk all ingredients together in a small bowl. Provide individual dipping bowls for each guest.

Pizza Party

Hostess Jennie Hampton, a Leader, is a South Carolina professional cook and wife, happily married to a man who will eat anything she puts in front of him. He is a wonderful cook also, so they designed their retirement home with entertaining in mind. They both love to host fancy multicourse plated meals but also very casual parties.

Theme: Pizza. A make-your-own pizza party is a great option for groups of people with different tastes. No need to compromise on toppings when you can make your own, ensuring everyone is happy and well fed. This is also a great format for a "drop in whenever" party where you don't expect everyone to sit down and eat together. People can make and eat their pizza whenever they are ready.

Decorations: I am not much for theme decorations, but it's not hard to find red-and-white tablecloths and festive napkins. Themed disposable bowls and plates make for easy cleanup and add to the festive feel. I put out one bowl of each item and refill as necessary so food isn't sitting out too long.

Entertainment: Making the pizza provides a great deal of entertainment on its own, but you can have a vote for the best dough thrower, most unusual toppings, or even a best pizza shape contest. Prizes can be a dough roller, pizza cutter, or even a pack of Tums for the most unusual toppings.

Menu: This party is easily modified from a "do it all yourself" format to letting others help out. I usually send an invite listing the stuff I will provide and tell people they are welcome to bring whatever extra toppings they want. Sometimes people offer to bring stuff off my list, which means one less thing for me to do.

Appetizers—Antipasto Platter

- Include olives, pepperoncini salad peppers, cherry tomatoes, mushrooms, strips of bell pepper or the small whole peppers, artichoke hearts, cheese cubes (provolone, parmesan, manchego, gouda, gorgonzola, fresh mozzarella, etc.), and sliced or cubed meats (salami, prosciutto, mortadella, etc.). Add some nuts like pistachios or walnuts, and some type of fruit (plums, figs) or some jam or marmalade. And of course have some bread (crosti, breadsticks, Italian baguette) and crackers and/or flatbread and olive oil. For a larger party, I might offer different flavored oils.

Beverages

- Lemonade and iced tea
- Wine/beer
- Prosecco

Pizza Station

- Dough—I usually make or buy dough so people just have to cut off a portion and roll it the way they want. I also have some premade crusts and flatbreads so all the options are covered. I set up a separate rolling station with flour and rolling pins to contain the potential mess.

- Toppings—Whatever you want, just make sure to have lots of choices.
- Sauces—red sauce, spicy red sauce, margarita sauce
- Cheeses—mozzarella, provolone, gruyere
- Spices—crushed red peppers, basil, oregano, salt, pepper, garlic salt
- Salad Bar—I use the salad bar for both an appetizer and a main course option. I just add extra topping options that might not go on pizzas (e.g., cucumbers, carrots, mandarin oranges, dried cranberries, grape tomatoes, crunchy onions, croutons).

Desserts

- For any event, I normally make or buy something chocolate, something not chocolate, and a fruit tray. I make "small bites" desserts since most people fill up on pizza and can't eat big desserts.

Recipes

BASIC PIZZA DOUGH

Ingredients

1½ tsp.	active dry yeast
1 oz.	warm water
7 oz.	bread flour
½ tsp.	salt
½ oz.	olive oil
1 tsp.	honey

Instructions

Stir yeast into water to dissolve.
Add flour.
Stir remaining ingredients into flour mixture.
Knead dough by hand or with a dough hook until smooth and elastic (about 5–7 minutes). Place dough into lightly greased bowl and cover. Place in warm location for 30 minutes.
Punch down dough and divide. Use immediately or wrap tightly and refrigerate up to 2 days.
Roll on lightly floured surface. Top as desired.
Bake at 400 degrees for 8–12 minutes.

BASIC PIZZA SAUCE

Ingredients

2 Tbsp.	olive oil
5 cloves	garlic, minced
28 oz.	diced tomatoes (canned are fine)
½ tsp.	salt
½ tsp.	oregano

Instructions

Sauté garlic in olive oil for 5–10 minutes. Add tomatoes, salt, and oregano.
Bring to a boil; reduce to a simmer and cook for 30 minutes.
Puree and strain if necessary.
Adjust seasonings to taste.

Taco Bar

Hostess Morgan Tyree, an Organizer. I love hosting informal gatherings where much of the work can be done ahead of time and then designing a setup where people can serve themselves. (And I'm all about simplicity and salsa—lots of salsa!)

189

Theme: Mexican. A great option for casual get-togethers, celebrations, and of course, fiestas! Also, it's easy to feed a large group and meet a variety of dietary needs.

Decorations: Use brightly colored napkins and tablecloths, cactus centerpieces, maracas, terra cotta pots, or a piñata (décor plus a game and dessert!). You can also have a lot of fun with the title—Taco 'bout a Party, Taco 'bout a Boy/Girl (baby shower), Taco 'bout a Couple (bridal shower), or you've always got Taco Tuesday/Thursday. The options are endless!

Entertainment: Pass around a sombrero filled with conversation-starter questions on pieces of paper. Create a salsa bar with a variety of salsas ranging in spice levels, and see who can handle the heat! Invite your guests to bring their favorite chips, salsa, or guacamole (brand or recipe), and have everyone vote for their favorite(s).

Menu: This is a "do it your way" menu. You may choose many or few of the options, buy most of them from the store, or make most of them from scratch (or anywhere in between). Your guests can go through the bar and make anything their heart desires—from a plate of nachos, to a taco salad, to yes, even a taco! I'm sharing my recipes for homemade salsa and taco seasoning. You will be able to find other specific Mexican recipes (such as flan or Mexican brownies) online or purchase them from a restaurant or store. The remainder of the items are easy to make, with very little prep involved. My kind of cooking!

Appetizer

- Tortilla chips, salsa, and guacamole

Beverages

- Limeade

- Sangria
- Margaritas

Taco Bar
(select the choices that will work best for your group)

- Taco shells, tostadas, tortillas (flour/corn)
- Meat of choice (ground beef, pulled pork, shredded chicken, fish, shrimp, tofu)
- Shredded cheese, sour cream, queso
- Chopped lettuce, black olives, diced tomatoes, jalapeños, avocados, corn
- Refried beans, black beans, pinto beans
- Spanish rice, cilantro-lime rice, potatoes
- Salsa, hot sauce, taco sauce, salad dressing, cilantro

Dessert

- Flan, Mexican brownies and ice cream, churros, or sopaipillas (I would personally just buy one or two of these and call dessert done!)

Recipes

HOMEMADE SALSA

Ingredients

4	10 oz. cans of diced tomatoes (I use a combination of Rotel brand tomatoes—Mexican, Fire Roasted, and Chipotle)
¼ c.	onion
1 Tbsp.	lime juice
	salt
2 Tbsp.	cilantro

Instructions

Combine all ingredients in a food processor and blend as much or as little as you'd like. Serve with tortilla chips. Makes a lot of salsa (about 40 oz.), which usually lasts the Tyree house about one week.

TACO SEASONING

Ingredients

1 Tbsp.	chili powder
½ tsp.	garlic powder
½ tsp.	paprika
1½ tsp.	cumin
1 tsp.	salt
1 tsp.	pepper

Instructions

In a small bowl, mix together all of the ingredients. Use however much you like (depending on your preference), and store in an airtight container.

conclusion

open your heart

Find out who you are and do it on purpose.

Dolly Parton

Thank you for joining me to chat about all things hospitality. I hope you felt cozy, cared for, and at home. Before our next get-together, I want you to promise me three things.

Promise me that you will welcome your hospitality personality with open arms.

Please don't waste a second wishing you were wired differently. Our world needs your *particular* and *perfect* gifts of hospitality. You have a unique and God-given way of interacting with others; don't fight against your tendencies. If you do, you'll only be limiting your potential reach, and wouldn't that be a disservice? You were specifically and individually created to effectively impact *your* circles of influence. Press into this truth. Seek out all the possibilities around you, and make sure to let your hospitality personality shine!

Promise me that you will name your habits, navigate your hurdles, and negotiate your hang-ups with hospitality (both in giving and receiving).

Knowing who you are and what you need to do (within your hospitality personality) will allow you to flourish as a host. Whether in your home or on the move, remember to use healthy hospitality guidelines. Commit to knowing the hospitality habits you want to keep and the ones you want to develop differently. Consider each hospitality hurdle (who, what, where, when, why) both directly and delicately. Create hosting times that minimize your hospitality hang-ups by intentionally orchestrating the details in the ways that help you feel the most at ease when hosting. Make it your mission to increase blessing and decrease stressing.

Promise me that you will look for opportunities to be hospitable: daily, weekly, monthly, seasonally, and yearly.

Leaders, Entertainers, Includers, and Organizers—open your heart to those God has placed in your life. Each one of your circles needs your time and attention; they need YOU. Schedule your hospitality, and don't forget to give away secret and spontaneous hospitality too—it's fun!

In her book *Daring to Be Yourself*, Alexandra Stoddard wisely says, "When you give your presence, you are giving the most. Ultimately, time is all you have. When you pay attention to someone else, you honor that person and the other person can honor you. You act not out of duty, but because you want to."[1]

Most of all, my friend, be yourself and share yourself—you are a gift.

notes

Chapter 1 Welcome!

1. Brené Brown, *Daring Greatly* (New York: Avery, 2012), 8.

Chapter 2 The Four Hospitality Personalities

1. Dictionary.com, s.v. "hospitality," accessed June 6, 2018, https://www.dic tionary.com/browse/hospitality?s=t.

2. Dictionary.com, s.v. "personality," accessed June 6, 2018, https://www.dic tionary.com/browse/personality?s=t.

Chapter 3 Setting

1. Betty Crocker, *Betty Crocker's Guide to Easy Entertaining* (Hoboken, NJ: Wiley, 1959), 8.

Chapter 5 Serving

1. Shauna Niequist, *Bread & Wine: A Love Letter to Life around the Table with Recipes* (Grand Rapids: Zondervan, 2013), 49.

2. Emmie Martin, "90% of Americans Don't Like to Cook—and It's Costing Them Thousands Each Year," *USA Today*, September 27, 2017, https://www.cnbc .com/2017/09/27/how-much-americans-waste-on-dining-out.html.

Chapter 6 Socializing

1. Kendra Cherry, "How You Can Tell That You're an Introvert," Very Well Mind, October 18, 2019, https://www.verywellmind.com/signs-you-are-an-intro vert-2795427.

2. Susan Cain, *Quiet: The Power of Introverts in a World That Can't Stop Talking* (New York: Crown Publishers, 2012), 2–3.

Chapter 7 Sharing

1. Katie M. Reid, *Made Like Martha: Good News for the Woman Who Gets Things Done* (New York: Waterbrook, 2018), 148.

Chapter 8 Who

1. Reese Witherspoon, *Whiskey in a Teacup: What Growing Up in the South Taught Me about Life, Love, and Baking Biscuits* (New York: Touchstone, 2018), 10.

Chapter 10 Where

1. Jessica N. Turner, *The Fringe Hours: Making Time for You* (Grand Rapids: Revell, 2015), 47–48.

Chapter 12 Why

1. Shasta Nelson, "Frientimacy: The 3 Requirements of All Healthy Friendships," YouTube, December 15, 2017, https://www.youtube.com/watch?v=hmJyWreER7A.notes.

2. Patricia S. York, "Why the Pineapple Became the Symbol of Hospitality," *Southern Living*, accessed January 19, 2019, https://www.southernliving.com/culture/pineapple-hospitality.

3. Alexandra Kuykendall, *Loving My Actual Neighbor: 7 Practices to Treasure the People Right in Front of You* (Grand Rapids: Baker Books, 2019), 193.

4. Theresa J. Borchard, "Understanding the Loneliness Epidemic," Psych Central, February 4, 2019, https://psychcentral.com/blog/understanding-the-loneliness-epidemic/.

Chapter 13 Connection

1. Kristen Hatton, "Hospitality Is . . . People Not Presentation," Kristen Hatton.com, January 7, 2017, https://www.kristenhatton.com/hospitality-people-not-presentation/.

2. Patricia Mendez, *Easy Entertaining for Beginners: You Can Throw a Fabulous Party, from a Holiday Fiesta to a Romantic Evening for Two* (Torrance, CA: Maple Heights Press, 2008), xv.

Chapter 15 Coziness

1. Myquillyn Smith, *Cozy Minimalist Home: More Style, Less Stuff* (Grand Rapids: Zondervan, 2018), 195.

Conclusion

1. Alexandra Stoddard, *Daring to Be Yourself* (New York: Doubleday, 1990), 295.

Morgan Tyree is a professional organizer (chaos calmer), writer (list lover), and fitness instructor (exercise enthusiast). She has a desire to help others be their best and to encourage and equip them in every season of life by inspiring intentionality. She runs her own personal organization and time-management business and lives with her husband, David, and their three children (affectionately termed their ABCs) in Colorado. Morgan invites you to join her on a peaceful path to simplicity. Connect with her online at www.morganizewithme.com.

Discover the Secret to Getting
MORE out of Your Day

If you've struggled to find balance and direction in your overloaded life, let Morgan's system help you discover the FREEDOM of less hustle and more HARMONY.

ℛ Revell
a division of Baker Publishing Group
www.RevellBooks.com

Available wherever books and ebooks are sold.

Connect with Morgan

MorganizeWithMe.com

Visit Morgan online and subscribe to her
email list to receive updates, tips
on organizing, and much more!

 MorganizeWithMe   @MorganizeWithMe

 @MorganizeWithMe   pinterest.com/morgantyree